Capital Investment Appraisal

Other Titles in this Series

Hoare **Project Management Using Network Analysis**
Hobbs **Control Over Inventory and Production**
Gorle and Long **Essentials of Product Planning**

Consulting Editorship: **Metra Consulting Group**

Other McGraw-Hill Management Manuals

Davis **The Organization of Training**
Margerison **Managing Effective Work Groups**
Drake and Smith **Behavioural Science in Industry**

Capital Investment Appraisal

Ian W. Harrison

Strategic Development Manager
Miles Druce & Co. Limited

London · New York · St Louis · San Francisco · Düsseldorf · Johannesburg
Kuala Lumpur · Mexico · Montreal · New Delhi · Panama · Paris · São Paulo
Singapore · Sydney · Toronto

Published by
McGRAW-HILL Book Company (UK) Limited
MAIDENHEAD · BERKSHIRE · ENGLAND

07 084426 7

Printed and bound in Great Britain

Contents

Preface

Capital expenditure is the use of today's funds to generate tomorrow's profits. As such it is the concern of managers at all levels, both line and staff, as well as management consultants and business academics. The importance of appraising capital investment efficiently, so as to make the best possible use of available capital, increases as industry becomes more capital-intensive and higher rates of interest make the 'time value' of money more important.

The object of this book is to provide the non-specialist manager with a basic understanding of the problems of capital investment appraisal and the techniques that are used to resolve these problems. The emphasis is on concepts rather than on technical details, the aim being to equip the reader to ask the right questions rather than to perform all the calculations himself. A certain familiarity with elementary algebraic notation and with elementary accounting terminology is assumed in the course of the book. The reader who takes fright at an algebraic equation or at a discussion of capital allowances and depreciation is advised to continue undaunted; neither is essential to the general argument.

I should like to express my thanks to my many friends and colleagues at Metra, at the University of Pennsylvania; at Miles Druce, who provided relevant and irrelevant advice; to several secretaries, particularly Marilyn Dalick and Myra Heron, who struggled with my handwriting; and to my wife, Janet, who provided moral support. The responsibility for errors, omissions, inaccuracies and shortcomings remains, of course, my own.

Ian W. Harrison

1 Basic concepts

There are essentially three distinct ways in which a company spends money: it pays taxes to the government; it pays interest and dividends to those who have provided capital for the company's operations; and it incurs expenses to pay its staff, purchase raw materials and equipment, and generally keep the company in business.

It is convenient to separate the expenses of a company into two categories: *operating expenditure,* which covers those items necessary for the day to day operations, such as wages and salaries, maintenance of equipment, and purchase of raw materials; and *capital investment expenditure,* which covers those items necessary to maintain the long-term growth of the company, such as building a new plant, purchasing the equipment for a new production line, carrying out research to improve an existing product or develop a new product, or launching an advertising campaign to promote a new product.

WHAT IS CAPITAL INVESTMENT?

In most cases the benefits obtained from operating expenditure (or at least the losses that would be suffered without the expenditure) are easy to define and measure: if salaries and wages are not paid, there will be no staff to operate the company; if new materials are not purchased, or if production equipment is not serviced and maintained, no production can take place. In each of these cases the benefits are not only easily definable and (at least in principle) measurable; they are also relatively short-term. Typically, they relate to periods of a few weeks or months at most.

For capital expenditure, on the other hand, the situation is rather different; the benefits resulting from the construction of a new plant, a research and development project, or a long-term advertising campaign, are considerably harder to determine precisely, as they depend on such factors as future demands for production, the success of a research project or the effect of an advertising campaign. Furthermore, the benefits will accrue over a considerably longer period of time; it may be several years before the benefits of a major capital expenditure project are fully realized.

The allocation of a given item of expenditure to *capital* or *operating* depends not only on the factors mentioned above, but also on the type of industry concerned. An expenditure whose benefits would accrue over a two-year period would be considered a capital investment if it is for the design of next year's dresses for a fashion house, but might be considered an operating expense if it is for the replacement of a set of valves in a power station.

For a typical company in a manufacturing industry, the cut-off point is frequently set at one year: expenses whose benefits will accrue over a period greater than one year are classed as a 'capital expenses', while those whose benefits accrue over a shorter period are regarded as 'operating expenses'. This distinction is also roughly consistent with that used for the calculation of corporation tax: operating expenses are (usually) fully allowable against tax as soon as they are incurred, while capital expenses are (usually) at best only allowable over a period of years (see chapter 3). Table 1.1 gives some examples of the two different types of expenditure for a small company in the light engineering industry.

Table 1.1

Capital	Operating
Purchase of a new machine tool	Wages and salaries
An advertising campaign	Raw materials
Improved safety measures to comply with new laws	Maintenance and servicing
Purchase of a painting for the chairman's office	Rent and rates
Installation of a computer for production and inventory control	Electricity, gas, water, telephone, etc.
Purchase of a patent for a new product	Office overhead expenses
Construction of an additional warehouse	
Research programme to improve a particular problem	

Because of the nature of capital investment—it has been defined as the use of today's funds to generate tomorrow's profits—it is obviously vitally important to the future growth and continued profitability of a company that capital investment decisions be made as wisely as possible. The analysis of the different possibilities for capital investment is called *capital investment appraisal*; the procedure for making decisions on the source of funds to be used for a given investment and the detailed timing of the investment is called *capital budgeting*. In this book we shall be concerned mainly with capital investment appraisal, and only peripherally with the more detailed questions of capital budgeting.

PROJECTS

In the usual terminology of capital investment appraisal, a single investment possibility is referred to as a *project*. Each of the examples of capital expenditure listed in the first column of Table 1.1 would thus be regarded as a capital investment project. With this terminology the object of capital investment appraisal is to provide a rule for deciding, in the case of any given capital investment project, whether the project should be undertaken or not.

In practice, of course, deciding what constitutes a project is not always a trivial question. A major project to enter a new line of business, may cover a number of different sub-projects, not all of which will be essential—e.g., acquisition of a subsidiary company manufacturing the product, construction of a new production line to make the product, modification of existing production facilities, launching an advertising campaign, recruitment of new personnel, etc. Some of these sub-projects may represent mutual alternatives, others may represent necessary parts of the main project.

For the moment, however, we shall assume that such cases either can always be reduced to one project (e.g., enter a new line of business), the choice of the best sub-projects representing a separate problem which is solved independently, or be considered as a collection of several mutually exclusive alternative projects (e.g., enter a new line of business *either* by acquiring company XYZ *or* by constructing a new production line), where the decision now is to accept either one or none of the two projects. This assumption is valid as long as no external constraints are imposed which might affect the projects. (Such a constraint would be: no matter what happens in other years, the company must be able to maintain its divided payments for the next two years; this might force acceptance of sub-projects which essentially trade off later profits for earlier, smaller profits.) In chapter 8 we shall discuss one method of dealing with such projects.

External Constraints

Project Cash Flows

In a classic article on stock market portfolio analysis (see Bibliography, 11), Harry Markowitz states: 'The process of selecting a portfolio may be divided into two stages. The first stage starts with observation and experience and ends with beliefs about the future performance of available securities. The second starts with the relevant beliefs about future performances and ends with the choice of portfolio.' In the capital investment case the situation is almost identical: if we substitute 'a set of investments' for 'portfolio', and 'cash flows associated with available projects' for 'performances of available securities', the statement holds exactly.

Capital investment appraisal is by definition concerned with the second of these two stages. The solution of the first stage, which depends on such techniques as cost accounting and forecasting, is a separate problem, some aspects of which are dealt with in companion volumes in this Series. In order to clarify the distinction between the two stages, we need to define precisely the interface between them—i.e., the set of figures which constitutes the output from stage one and the input to stage two. The output from stage one—the basic financial information about a project which has to be assembled before the appraisal stage can begin—consists simply of the forecast cash flows associated with the project during its life: the actual extra income and expenditure which would result from acceptance of the project.

The basic rules for determining the cash flows associated with a given investment project may be stated very simply:

Determine the life of the project—i.e., that period of time after which the effects of the project under consideration may reasonably be ignored, and divide this life into suitable time periods. For a project with a ten-year life (e.g., construction of a new plant), division into ten one-year periods would probably be the most appropriate for determining the cash flows; for a project with a one-year life (e.g., an advertising campaign), the periods should be quarters or even months. In most practical cases, however, annual periods are sufficiently accurate, and unless otherwise stated all examples in this book will use annual periods. For consistency it is convenient to refer to the year in which the project is commissioned as 'year 0', and subsequent years as 'year 1', 'year 2', and so on.

For each time period, determine the actual incremental cash flow which would result from the project if it were accepted. These cash flows are usually most conveniently determined in three component parts: capital expenditure, operating expenditure, and revenue.

Two important points need to be emphasized:

Only *actual* cash flows representing expenditure by the company or income to the company are included; fictitious cash flows such as depreciation (which is a transfer of funds within the company) should be omitted.

The cash flows are *incremental*; only those cash flows which would result from the decision to go ahead with the project are included. If, for example, a company has already decided to build a new factory costing £200 000, and is considering a further capital investment project to install an additional production line in the new factory which would increase the cost to £250 000, then the capital expense attributable to the capital investment project is £250 000 – £200 000 = £50 000, since the remaining £200 000 is already committed. Strictly, the cash flows should be determined as follows: calculate the total cash receipts and expenditures of the company (i) if the project were accepted, and (ii) if the project were not accepted. The difference between (i) and (ii) is then the incremental (or marginal) cash flow attributable to the project. Although it is rarely necessary actually to calculate both sets of cash flows, this rule does give a precise method of evaluation.

Note No reference has been made in the above discussion to problems of taxation, capital allowances, or investment grants. For the present, we shall consider an environment which is completely tax-free, the modifications necessary to take these factors into account being discussed in chapter 3. In addition, it has been assumed that all future cash flows can be forecast exactly. Despite the obvious limitations of this assumption, we shall defer discussion of questions of risk and uncertainty until chapter 7.

Two Case Studies

The following case studies illustrate the calculation of the project cash flows.

Table 1.2 *Extension of product range: Calculation of cash flows (£'000s)*

Year	0	1	2	3	4	5	6	7	8
1. Sales ('000 units)	0	10	15	18	20	23	25	28	0
2. Capital expenditure	400	70	0	0	0	0	0	0	0
3. Revenue	0	250	375	438	500	563	625	688	50
4. Fixed costs	0	30	30	30	30	30	30	30	0
5. Variable production costs	0	150	200	225	250	275	300	325	0
6. Total operating costs (4 + 5)	0	180	230	255	280	305	330	355	0
7. Net trading profit (3 – 6)	0	70	145	183	220	258	295	333	50
8. Net cash flows (7 – 2)	–400	0	145	183	220	258	295	333	50

Notes:

(i) taxation is, for the moment, ignored;
(ii) the revenue from the scrap value of the factory and plant is assumed to come in during the year after production has finished;
(iii) depreciation, of course, does not appear as a cash flow.

The ABC company manufactures 'own brand' household appliances for several department store chains. They are considering extending their product range to include new lines. This would be achieved by building a new factory at a total capital cost of £470 000, £400 000 in year 0, and £70 000 in year 1. Fixed costs of operating the factory, which would commence operations at the beginning of year 1 (one year after commissioning) are estimated at £30 000 per year; these include such items as rent, rates, building maintenance, etc. The marketing department estimates gross sales of the new lines to be 10 000 units in year 1, 15 000 units in year 2, and a constant increase of 2500 units per year thereafter; the proposed sales price is £25 per unit. Production costs are estimated at £15 per unit for the first 10 000 units and £10 per unit thereafter. The life of the project is considered to be seven years from the start of production, and the factory and plant are to be sold off after that for £50 000. Table 1.2 shows how the net cash flows for each year are calculated.

In addition to their above-mentioned project, the ABC company is also considering the following cost reduction proposal from their production division. Recent technological developments in process control would enable manufacturing costs on two major production lines to be reduced from £10 per unit to £8 per unit. The process control equipment, including installation, would cost £100 000 (all incurred in year 0), but in order to use the equipment a small part of the existing production line machinery would also have to be replaced, at a cost of £20 000 (incurred in

Table 1.3 *Project control project: Calculation of cash flows (£'000s)*

Year	0	1	2	3	4	5	6
1. Sales ('000 units)		10	11	12	13	14	15
2. Capital expenditure	100	20	0	0	0	0	0
3. Savings on fixed production costs		1	1	1	1	1	1
4. Revenue from sale of old machines		3	0	0	0	0	0
5. Savings in variable production costs		20	22	24	26	28	30
6. Total net savings (3 + 4 + 5)		24	23	25	27	29	31
7. Net cash flow (6 – 2)	–100	4	23	25	27	29	31

Notes:

(i) since the installation of the new equipment would not take more than a few weeks, we can assume the capital expenditure to take place during the first year of operation (year 1, rather than year 0).

year 1). However, the old machines would realize £3000 if sold for scrap, and the replacement should save £1000 per year in maintenance costs.

Total sales are forecast at 10 000 units in year 1, increasing by 1000 in each subsequent year, and the total life of the equipment is estimated at six years with no significant resale value at the end of that time. Table 1.3 shows how the cash flows are calculated.

WHO MAKES DECISIONS?

Before we go on to examine how capital investment decisions should be made, we should examine two organizational questions. Who is going to make such decisions? How should the information be controlled and organized to facilitate good decision-making?

At the extreme ends of the spectrum of capital investment projects the answer to the first question is obvious: few companies would not give a local plant manager authority to decide on a £50 expenditure for a new vacuum cleaner for the factory, and probably no company would make below board level a £15 million decision to build a new plant. The problems arise at the middle of the spectrum. How should you determine cut-off levels for capital expenditure responsibility of intermediate management, and how do you set up a system sufficiently flexible to cope with most, if not all, eventualities?

As long as the quality of decision-making is not impaired, it is evident that the lower the level at which it takes place the better: there is no point in using the time of a highly paid senior executive to make decisions which could equally well have been made by a junior manager earning one-third of the senior's salary. So the question to be answered is: When will the quality of decision-making be impaired if decisions are delegated? There are essentially two reasons for bad decision-making. Either the information available to the decision-maker is incorrect or incomplete, or the decision-maker fails to process the information correctly.

Given a properly implemented control system, where the methods of information collection and processing, together with the appropriate criteria for decision-making, are defined clearly and unambiguously for all management, there is no inherent reason why a junior manager should be any more likely than his superiors to process information incorrectly. If this argument is accepted, the only possible reason for making decisions at a superior level is that the senior manager has access to information which is unavailable to his juniors.

Such information might fall into one of several categories: information relating to capital requirements of other divisions of the company, to external financial factors such as the cost to the company of borrowing money externally, or to overall policy decisions of the company—e.g., to expand one particular division at the expense of another. As a general rule, provided an efficient and standardized method of appraisal is used, capital investment decisions should be taken at the lowest level of management at which all the relevant information is available. In practice, the information usually lacking at a junior level is concerned with how the available capital should be allocated between different divisions of the company. (Note that the process of deciding on this allocation is sometimes known as 'capital budgeting', the resulting allocation being called a 'capital budget'; this is a slightly different usage from the definition given earlier in this chapter.)

The actual level of authority for expenditure given to any departmental divisional manager thus depends on the extent to which different departments or divisions are competing for capital funds (and, in practice, on the confidence the senior management has in the junior's ability to carry out standard appraisal methods), and it is impossible to lay down hard-and-fast rules for use in all companies. A rough guide might be: all projects involving total capital expenditure greater than 3 per cent of the average annual capital expenditure of a particular division must be justified according to standard procedures. If the total capital expenditure on a project exceeds 20 per cent of the average annual capital expenditure of that division, then the project must be referred to higher management for a final decision. In practice such rules should be defined precisely, and reviewed annually to ensure that they always permit the maximum delegation possible.

Where, among senior management, should these decisions be taken? The answer to this question is simple. Capital investment appraisal is concerned with the trade-off between present cash and future profits, and as such it forms unequivocally a part of the planning operations of the company; and therefore the responsibility for capital investment decisions belongs ultimately with that for corporate and financial planning, whether the appropriate individual is the planning manager, the financial director, or the managing director.

In practice, a typical procedure is for the planning department to supervise and assist with the preparation of all requests for capital above a certain size. If the expenses are sufficiently large to fall outside the responsibility of local divisional management, the planning department prepares and collates all relevant information for all competing projects. The ultimate decision is made by the planning manager, financial director, managing director, or by the full board of directors, depending on the division of planning responsibility within the company, and, of course, on the magnitude and importance of each individual project.

OUTLINE OF CAPITAL INVESTMENT APPRAISAL SYSTEM

The flow chart in Fig. 1.1 shows a typical (simplified) decision-making process for capital investment appraisal. The planning department has prepared a standardized pro-forma (see Fig. 1.2) to use when requesting authority for capital expenditure, and has defined cut-off levels for responsibility of divisional managers, as well as standard procedures for use in decision-making in all cases.

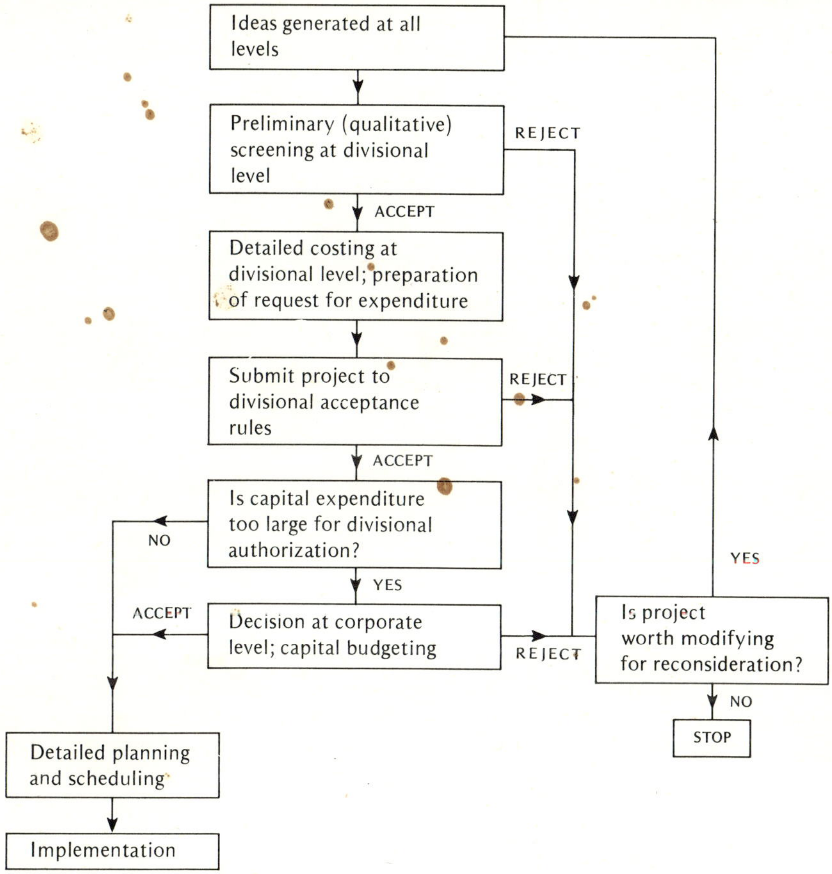

Fig. 1.1 *How investment decisions are made.*

A proposal for a project involving capital expenditure may originate anywhere in the organization. On origination each proposal is considered informally within the relevant division. If the project is considered to be feasible, the divisional staff, with assistance from the planning department where necessary, prepare forecast cash flows for the project and complete the standard pro-forma request for expenditure. The completed pro-forma is then submitted for formal departmental consideration. If it satisfies the general guidelines laid down by the corporate planning for that division, the project is accepted at divisional level. If the capital required is within

Request for capital expenditure authorization, XYZ Ltd					
Division:			Project title:		
Description:					
Year	0 (1973)	1 (1974)	2 (1975)	3 (1976)	4 (1977)
Capital expenditure					
Capital allowances					
Investment grants					
Marginal operating profit					
Scrap value					
Other requirements and constraints:					
Prepared by:				Date:	

Fig. 1.2 *Simplified capital expenditure form.*

limits for authorization within the division, it goes ahead to detailed planning and implementation. If it is too large, it goes to corporate level for approval.

The planning department, headed by the director responsible for planning, normally considers all proposed projects once annually. On the basis of their decisions, and those made at divisional level during the preceding year, the department prepares annually a capital budget for five years, showing all commitments to capital expenditure for the next five years, by quarter for year 1, and annually for years 2–5. Projects approved at the corporate level are returned to the appropriate division for detailed planning and scheduling for implementation. Projects rejected at any level are returned to their point of origin for re-appraisal, in order to see whether changes in the project would increase its attractiveness to the company.

Even when the annual capital budget has been finalized, the appraisal procedure has not terminated. The budget is updated quarterly, actual cash flows being compared with the forecasts. If the deviations are sufficient to lower substantially the attractiveness of a given project, the possibility of cancelling the project and writing off the expended capital, or of modifying the project, is considered. For all significant variations of actual figures from forecasts the reasons for the discrepancy are examined by the same people who prepared the forecasts, this control of actual against forecast figures enabling the accuracy of forecasting to be continuously improved.

At the end of each yearly cycle, all existing projects are re-appraised at divisional or corporate level as appropriate, and only if the project is still sufficiently attractive is continuation authorized for subsequent years.

The above description shows in outline how such a system may operate. The description is necessarily sketchy, for the construction of this type of system falls within more general problems of corporate planning, which go beyond the scope of this book. We shall, however, return to some aspects of the subject in chapter 8.

Checklist

1. Can you define, and distinguish between, capital expenditure and operating expenditure? Give five examples of each from your own company.
2. Draw up a chart showing the different authority levels for capital expenditure in your company. In the light of the discussion in this chapter, do you think these levels are satisfactory?
3. Figure 1.2 shows a simplified capital expenditure request form. Does your company use such a form? If not, can you design a suitable one?

2
Financial factors

In order to be able to make effective decisions about the acceptance or rejection of capital investment projects, it is obviously necessary to know how much capital is available for investment. This implies a knowledge not only of the amount of capital actually on hand in the form of cash or readily realizable assets, but also of what other possible sources of capital exist, how much it would cost to raise capital from these sources, and what other decisions (such as dividend policy) may influence future capital availability.

SOURCES OF CASH IN HAND

For a typical company, Fig. 2.1 shows the principal financial interactions relevant to capital investment decisions. Capital investments must be paid for out of 'cash in hand' (cash plus any assets easily convertible into cash); these investments generate a net trading cash flow (the sum of the individual incremental cash flows defined in chapter 1 for each project undertaken). This, after deduction of financial charges (interest on loans raised for capital investment, etc.), gives trading profit, which in turn, after taking out tax and depreciation, produces net profits. Net profits are split into dividends to shareholders and retained profits, which together with depreciation, go back into cash in hand. Cash in hand can also be increased by raising loans, or by issuing new equity capital. After making repayments of existing loans, the residual cash in hand represents the amount of money available for capital investment, thus completing the cycle.

We have now identified three distinct sources of cash in hand which can be used for investment purposes:

(a) Internally generated capital, consisting of depreciation and retained profits.

(b) Loans, that is, capital made available to the company from outside sources in return for agreed interest payments and (usually) a specified schedule of repayment.

(c) Equity issues, where money is raised from outside sources in return for a share in future profits.

In order to understand more fully the impact that these different sources of capital may have on capital investment decisions, it is necessary to examine first in rather more detail the mechanics of raising money from each source.

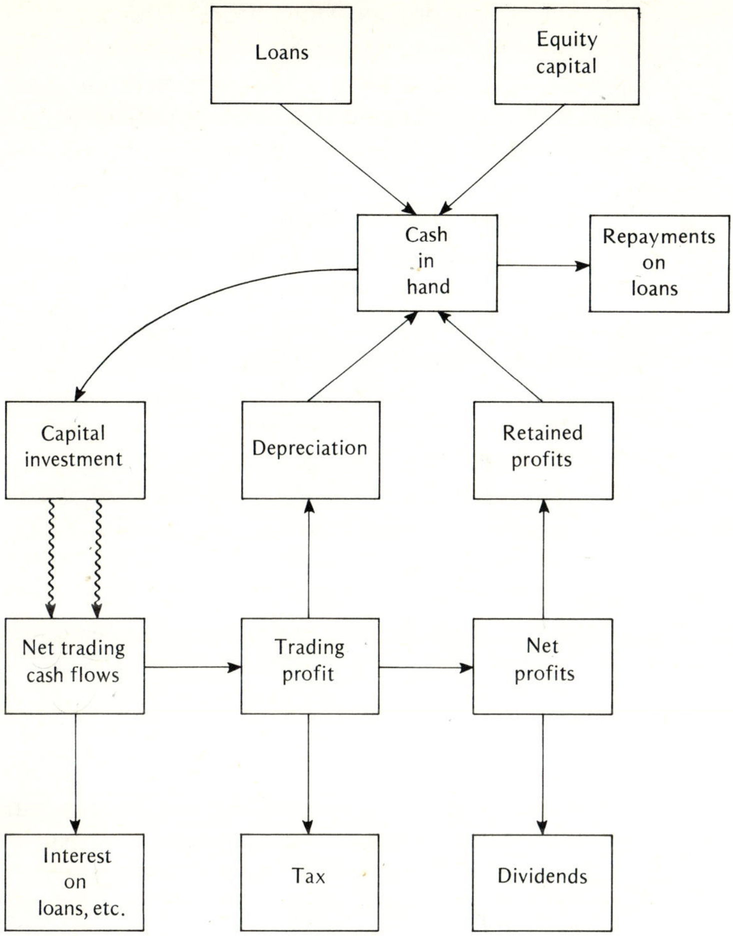

Fig. 2.1 *Principal financial interactions of a company making capital investments.*

Internally Generated Capital

Internally generated capital derives from two different sources: depreciation, and retained profits. It is important to realize, however, that this distinction is to some extent arbitrary.

Depreciation is a transfer of funds from one account to another within the company, and does not represent an actual cash flow out of the company. It is standard accounting practice to regard the depreciation of capital assets associated with a particular project as direct expense to be charged to that project, the primary reason being to spread out the capital cost over the life of the asset in which the capital was invested. Although, as stated in chapter 1, this should not be taken as a direct expense attributable to a project for purposes of capital investment appraisal (since it is not an actual cash flow), it is nevertheless normal practice to deduct depreciation expenses before calculating net profits. Thus, depreciation must be regarded as an internal generation of capital, although, from the point of view of potential investment, a pound generated from depreciation is no different from a pound retained from earnings.

Net profits, after deduction of depreciation and corporation tax, are the ultimate profits made by the company. All deductions have been made and the company has the choice of determining the proportion to be paid out as dividends to the shareholders and the proportion to be retained for reinvestment within the company. In practice, this choice is usually made as much on the basis of past history and future expectations as on the actual profits in a given year. It is considered by many companies (and doubtless by many shareholders) to be a sign of weakness and incompetent management ever to pay a lower dividend than was paid the preceding year. Hence, the guiding principle is often: Pay the same dividend as last year if possible; increase the dividend if net profits have increased, but not if it may be impossible to maintain the increase in subsequent years.

From the shareholders' point of view, this type of policy may not be the most profitable. If the possibilities for reinvestment within the company are particularly good in a given year, it may be to the shareholders' advantage to receive lower dividends, because, in terms of increased share price and increased dividends in future years, the return on investment obtained by the company will more than compensate the shareholder for his loss of dividends. Conversely, if there are few capital investment possibilities open to the company, the shareholder may be able to make better use of the money himself, and it would therefore be to his interest to have a high dividend paid out.

At least in theory, the proportion of net profits retained for reinvestment in a given year should be regarded as a control on the amount of capital available for investment, and before deciding on proportion of profits to be retained, the possible applications of retained capital should be examined.

Loans

A loan is defined as an arrangement whereby capital is made available to the company in return for an agreed interest rate and (usually) an agreed schedule of repayments. Loans may be made by a bank, an individual, the government, etc., but whoever is the source of the capital, the interest rate and schedule of repayments will depend essentially on two factors: the current state of the market for money, and the degree of risk inherent in the loan. The interest paid to the lender may be regarded as compensation for the risk that the company may not be able to repay the loan (because there is always a possibility that a company will go bankrupt or at least be unable to repay the loan on schedule), as well as compensation to the lender for depriving him of the use of the capital for the period of the loan.

In order to protect himself as far as possible against the possibility of a borrower defaulting on all or part of a loan, a potential lender will normally want to know what the capital is to be used for, so that he can make his own judgement about the likelihood of the project's generating enough income to ensure payment of interest and repayment of the loan. This means that in many cases the ability to raise a loan from a bank, for example, and the interest rate paid on the loan, may depend on the nature of the specific project or projects for which the loan capital is required. Even where the ability to raise a loan may not depend on a specific project—a bank overdraft or a 'bridging loan', for example—the lender will obviously be influenced in his decisions by the overall financial position of the company. In particular, he may be unwilling to lend capital for any purpose if the ratio of total debts to total assets already exceeds that which is considered normal for the industry in which the company is operating.

In summary, the loan possibilities available for a company will depend on the amount of money generally available in the market, the project(s) for which the loan is required, and the overall financial position of the company.

A particular type of loan which deserves special mention is a debenture issue. This is the sale by a company to the general public of a type of bond; purchase of a bond entitles the bondholder to a fixed interest rate for a defined period of time and redemption (repurchase) by the company at an agreed price (usually the original purchase price, or a price close to it) at the end of that period of time. Two features of a debenture issue as a means of raising money are:

(a) The interest rate is offered by the company to potential purchasers, as opposed to being agreed mutually by borrower and lender.

(b) The precise purpose for which the capital is to be used need not be specified (although debenture purchasers are obviously easier to find when evidence is provided to convince them of the continued profitability of the company). This feature of debentures may give the company greater freedom than would be the case with bank loans.

Equity Issues

The third principal source of capital available to a company is new equity capital. The company sells additional shares (usually in the form of a 'rights issue' whereby existing shareholders are given the right to subscribe for new shares in the company at a price somewhat below the prevailing market price), undertaking only to give the purchasers the same dividend rights as existing shareholders. The existing corporation tax structure makes this method of raising new capital for investment relatively unattractive, essentially because shareholders are liable for income tax on dividends received, and corporation tax has been paid already on net profits of the company before payment of dividends. The net effect of this is effectively to impose a much higher rate of tax on income from shareholdings than, say, on income from debenture-holdings (see chapter 3).

Apart from the tax problems, there are other restrictions on the use of new equity issues as a means of raising capital. For 'political' reasons, the board of directors of a company usually does not like to make equity issues too frequently or for too small amounts. In addition, the cost of such an issue is heavily dependent on the current share price of the company, a quantity which may change rapidly with little or no warning. Thus, a sudden slump in the stock market can turn a new equity issue from a highly attractive prospect to one of doubtful worth.

Other forms of equity issues, such as preference shares and convertible loan stock or debentures, belong to the subject of company finance and the reader is referred for detailed analysis to textbooks on that subject.

THE PROBLEM OF COST OF CAPITAL

For capital raised through loans or equity issues, it is clear that there is a direct cost associated with obtaining the capital: interest on loans, and dividends on new shares issued. This cost is readily definable (although, at least for equity issues, not always readily calculable), and, in the case where the capital is raised specifically for a particular project, should be treated as a cost of the project. More precisely, the cash flows associated with making the loan (capital *in*; interest, dividends, and capital repayment *out*) should be calculated explicitly and added to the cash flows resulting from the project. The example below shows how these cash flows associated with raising capital are calculated.

Where the capital is generated internally or where externally generated capital is available for a number of projects, the problem of assigning a cost to the capital which can be applied to a project becomes rather more complex. Even in the case of internally generated capital there is an 'opportunity cost' associated with using the capital for an investment project; the capital could always be invested elsewhere (e.g., in a bank deposit account) and, by deciding to invest the capital in an investment project, a decision is made to forego the income from some such alternative source. In the case of loans or new equity capital not tied to a specific project, there are of course direct costs associated with raising the capital, and these have somehow to be taken into account in evaluating the attractiveness of a prospective investment project. The most satisfactory techniques available for solving these problems are those of discounted cash flow and are discussed in some detail in chapter 5.

Example of Different Methods of Finance

LMN Ltd is a medium-sized company whose principal business is mining and refining a variety of metals. In order to exploit a newly found deposit of ore, the company requires £5 million capital. This capital will be used for the purchase of equipment, construction of access facilities to the mine, and commencement of mining operations. No capital is available inside the company, but there are three alternative methods of raising the capital outside:

Method (*a*) A £5 million debenture issue at 8 per cent interest rate, repayable after 10 years.

Method (*b*) A loan of £5 million from a merchant bank at 9 per cent annual interest rate, repayable in 10 annual instalments of £500 000, beginning 1 year after the date of loan.

Method (*c*) An equity issue of 2.5 million new 25p shares at the current market price of £2. Dividends this year will be 10p per share (40 per cent), and long-term company policy is to increase dividends by 2.5p per nominal 25p share per year.

To compare these three sources of capital, we need first to calculate the cash flows that would result from raising the necessary capital from each source. In each case there is a positive (inward) cash flow of £5 million in year 0, representing receipt of the capital. The negative (outward) cash flows representing repayment of principal (in cases (a) and (b)) and interest (dividend payments) in subsequent years, however, vary substantially from source to source.

Method (*a*) Repayment of principal: one payment of £5 million in year 10. Annual interest payment: £400 000 in years 1, 2, 3, . . . 10. This can conveniently be summarized in the following table.

Year	0	1	2	3	4	5	6	7	8	9	10
Net cash flow (£'000s)	+5000	−400	−400	−400	−400	−400	−400	−400	−400	−400	−5400

Method (*b*) Repayment of principal: £500 000 in years 1, 2, 3, ... 10. Annual interest payment £5 million at 9 per cent = £450 000 in year 1. £4.5 million x 0.09 = £405 000 in year 2, etc., the interest decreases by £45 000 each year to £45 000 in year 10. This enables us to construct a similar table as follows.

Year	0	1	2	3	4	5	6	7	8	9	10
Net cash flow (£'000s)	+5000	−950	−905	−860	−815	−770	−725	−680	−635	−590	−545

Method (*c*) Repayment of principal is not relevant, since the 'lender' (purchaser of shares) has acquired a permanent holding in the company. However, the capital is not obtained for nothing, since dividends must be paid each year on each of 2.5 million additional shares. Assuming that the company maintains its policy of increasing dividends by 2.5p per share per year, this will result in an extra payment of 2.5 million x 10p = £250 000 in year 1, increasing by 2.5 million x 2.5p = £62 500 per year thereafter.

The annual cash flow will therefore be as shown in the following table.

Year	0	1	2	3	4	5	6	7	8	9	10
Net cash flow (£'000s)	+5000	−250	−312.5	−375	−437.5	−500	−526.5	−625	−687.5	−750	−812.5

Note that, unlike methods (a) and (b), the additional cash flows resulting from raising the capital from a new equity issue do not terminate after 10 years, but continue indefinitely.

In the above case study taxation has been ignored; we shall return to this case study to investigate the effects of taking taxation into account in chapter 3.

Checklist

1. What are the principal sources of cash for capital investment available to a company? What are the main advantages and disadvantages of each of these sources?
2. What cost of capital does (or should) your company use in considering capital investment projects?

3
Taxation and capital allowances

In chapter 1 we distinguished three ways in which a company spends money; one of these ways was payment of taxes to the government. (In fact, the cash flows between a company and the government are not exclusively oneway; certain types of investment grants are payable to the company by the government in the form of cash payments.) Since a company pays a substantial proportion of its profits to the government in the form of taxes, it is important, when considering a capital investment project, to consider what proportion of the initial capital expenditure may be reimbursed by the government, in one form or another, and what proportion of future profits, generated by the project, will be paid to the government. The purpose of this chapter is to examine the different forms of cash flows between company and government, to discuss in what circumstances these factors may affect capital investment decisions, and, where appropriate, how these factors may be taken into account.

A CAUTIONARY NOTE

Before discussing in detail the different types of taxation, allowances and grants that exist, a word of caution is necessary: the rates and structure of the tax system are complex and subject to frequent change, as governments and prevailing economic conditions change. The precise regulations for determining tax liability and grant eligibility are extremely complicated and may also change, while from time to time there may be fundamental reforms in the whole taxation system—e.g., the introduction of corporation tax in 1966, and the revisions to take effect from 1973.

This chapter contains a highly simplified description of the situation in effect in the UK at the time of writing, but before making use of any of the specific information contained here, care should be taken to verify that no alterations have taken place. However, it is to be hoped that our description of the basic methods will remain correct, and that the reader can see for himself what modifications will be necessary in the light of subsequent changes.

TAX—ASSOCIATED CASH FLOWS

There are at present five principal categories of payments and allowances between companies and government in the UK at the present time: income tax, value added tax (VAT), corporation tax, purchase tax, customs and excise duty, and capital allowances. (Capital gains tax is not a separate tax on companies, but chargeable gains are taken into account when computing corporation tax liability.)

One of these categories, income tax, applies only to companies which trade as individuals or partnerships. Such companies are then subject to taxation under the income tax provision of the Income and Corporation Taxes Act, 1970. Although one of the effects of the corporation tax legislation has been to encourage this form of trading in certain cases, the bulk of companies trade as limited companies, and as such are subject to corporation tax, not income tax. Hence, the liability of companies to income tax will not be considered in this book.

Of the other main categories, VAT and corporation tax generate cash flows from a company to the government. Capital allowances also generate government-to-company cash flows—but with one peculiar characteristic, because these are allowances and are 'paid' in the form of reductions in taxes. Thus, if the company is paying no tax, it gets no capital allowances. The following paragraphs discuss these cash flows in more detail.

Value Added Tax

Value added tax (VAT) is essentially a sales tax, payable by the ultimate consumer of a product. It is collected, however, at various points along the path from raw material to consumer: whenever a company buys materials, processes them, and sells them at a higher price, VAT is collected on 'the value added' and the tax reclaimed from the purchaser. The following example (which assumes a 10 per cent rate for VAT) shows in outline how the system works.

A company buys a semi-finished product for £10, and pays in addition £1 VAT, making £11 in total. The product is now processed and sold for £15, plus £1.50 VAT, making £16.50 in total. The £1.50 VAT is collected by the company from the purchaser, £1 of this being 'reimbursement' for the £1 paid on the purchased materials, while the remaining 50p represents the 10 per cent VAT on the £5 of 'value added' to the product and is paid to the government.

VAT has no effect on the principles of capital investment appraisal, but will affect the cash flows associated with any given project. In particular, the following points should be noted:

(a) VAT will be payable in general on all goods purchased; any goods that are necessary for a project therefore have their effective cost increased by the amount of VAT.

(b) VAT is chargeable on 'value added' by the company; in any project which changes the total value added by the company (by producing a higher priced product or more of an existing product, for example) will result in increased payment of VAT. This must be taken into account in determining the cash flows associated with the project.

(c) Where there is investment in stocks and work in progress associated with a project, cash will be needed to finance the payment of VAT on purchased materials, as this must be paid out before the 'reimbursement' when the product is sold. Where stocks are held for a long time this may be substantial and should be taken into account in determining the cash flows.

Corporation Tax

The most important form of taxation for most UK companies is corporation tax. This is a flat rate (at the time of writing, 40 per cent) tax levied on the trading profits of the company, after deduction of financial charges (interest on outstanding debts), operating expenses, and certain capital allowances (described on p. 22). From 1973, corporation tax is levied at a higher rate, with an 'imputation' system whereby shareholders are permitted to credit some of the tax paid by the company against their personal tax liabilities; these changes affect dividend policies, but not the techniques described in this book. All the examples in the book assume a 40 per cent rate for corporation tax, but are equally valid *as examples,* with obvious modifications, at any other tax rates. There are two important characteristics of corporation tax which may affect capital investment decisions:

(a) The tax is assessed on profits earned by the company in its complete accounting year. Losses in a particular accounting year may be carried forward to offset profits in future years, or back (one year only) to offset profits already earned, in which case the tax paid is then reclaimed. Thus, the precise timing of an investment project will determine in which accounting year the expenses fall. In addition to the obvious effects on timing of tax payments, the provision for carrying losses back at most one year may affect the magnitude of allowances which can be claimed.

(b) Unlike income tax (and corporation tax in many countries), corporation tax for the UK is not paid on a 'PAYE' basis. The tax assessed on a given accounting year does not become payable until the end of a fixed period following the last day of the accounting year. This period varies from company to company, and may be as short as nine months. If however the company was already in existence when corporation tax was introduced (in April 1966), the time lag may be extended to as much as twenty months.

This means that the cash flows representing corporation tax payment are out of step with the cash flows representing the profits on which the tax is calculated. For a project with uneven cash flows, this will result in correspondingly uneven tax payments, which may affect the feasibility or desirability of a venture. This is made clear in the example in Table 3.1.

Table 3.1

Year	0	1	2	3
Pre-tax profits	+1000	0	+1000	0
Tax payments	0	–400	0	–400
Post-tax profits	+1000	–400	+1000	–400

Thus, a project which has always positive pre-tax cash flows can actually produce negative post-tax cash flows in certain years.

Capital Allowances

One distinction between operating expenditure and capital expenditure is that the former is (with certain minor exceptions) fully allowable against tax immediately, whereas capital expenses are usually allowable only over a period of some years. In the UK, as in most other countries, the government considers that industries should be given some incentive to use their retained earnings and other sources of capital for investment, rather than paying all of it to shareholders. One mechanism for providing this incentive is to allow portions of certain types of capital expenditure to be deducted from (or allowed against) the trading profits before corporation tax is calculated. These portions of capital expenditure are called 'capital allowances'.

It is important not to confuse capital allowances with depreciation. Depreciation can be viewed in two ways: as the wastage of the capital actually used for an investment, or, alternatively, as the writing down or reduction in book value of capital assets carried out in order to 'lay aside' capital for future investment needs. Although it appears in the profit and loss statement as an expense (and in the balance sheet as a transfer from capital assets to liquid assets), it does not represent an actual cash flow, since no money physically leaves the company. In many countries (e.g., the USA and France) the capital allowances are precisely the amount by which capital assets are written down for depreciation, and in this case the method of calculating depreciation is fairly strictly controlled by regulation. In the UK, capital allowances and depreciation are quite separate, and while accountants are within reason permitted to calculate depreciation in any way which suits them, the method of calculation of capital allowances is precisely specified.

In the UK the method for calculating capital allowances was changed in the 1971 Finance Act. The method was considerably simplified so that it involved just two steps. First, an allowance may be made for an asset in the first year of its life. This is called the 'first year allowance'. For plant and machinery not installed in a 'development area' the first year allowance is 60 per cent*. In the case of plant installed in development areas (and also for ships) this rate is 100 per cent (i.e., the whole value of the asset can be offset against profits, for the purpose of tax calculations, in the first year of that asset's life). Secondly, a 'writing down' allowance may be claimed for an asset at a fixed rate on a 'reducing balance' basis in all years subsequent to the first. This means that the allowance is computed as a percentage of the original value of the asset minus the sum of the allowances made up to that time. A rate of 25 per cent on a reducing balance basis is allowed for plant and machinery. Of course, this may not apply to plant and machinery in a development area, since the whole value can be allowed in the first year.

Because of a shortage of profits, the company may not wish to claim a deduction of as much as 60 per cent (or 100 per cent) of the capital expenditure incurred in the first year, and it has the option therefore of disclaiming the first year allowance—in whole or in part—if it is to its advantage to do so. Such a disclaimer does, of course, have the effect of increasing the amount upon which the writing down allowance may be claimed in subsequent years.

For ships, the rule is slightly different, in that the first-year allowance of 100 per cent may be postponed rather than disclaimed. The amount postponed may be claimed in any subsequent year, or

* In the 1972 Finance Act, the government introduced 'free depreciation' as a temporary measure to encourage capital investment. This means that, at present, 100 per cent of any capital expenditure on plant and machinery can be claimed as a 'first-year allowance'. It seems likely, however, that in the near future there will be a return to the system described on this page.

years, thus allowing the company complete flexibility in making use of the relief.

When an item of plant is sold or scrapped, the proceeds (if any) are deducted from the reducing balance brought forward and the difference can be claimed in that year as a 'balancing' allowance. If the sale proceeds exceed the amount brought forward, the company is charged corporation tax on the excess as part of its profits, and no further allowances are given on that expenditure.

On some types of investment—in particular, industrial buildings—the writing down allowance is not calculated on a reducing balance basis (as used for plant and machinery). Instead a 'straight line' method is used. This simply means that a fixed percentage of the initial cost of the asset is allowed in every year; the allowance is therefore the same in each year. The rate for industrial buildings is, for example, 4 per cent; in addition, a so-called 'initial allowance' is given in the year of expenditure, amounting to 30 per cent in a development area and 15 per cent elsewhere.

Table 3.2

	(£)
Total cost	1000
Year 1: first year allowance	600
balance	400
Year 2: writing down allowance	100
balance	300
Year 3: writing down allowance	75
balance	225
Year 4: writing down allowance	56
balance	169
less scrap value	100
balancing allowance	69

Table 3.2 shows how capital allowances are calculated in a specific case. A company purchases a new machine for £1000; the machine has a useful life of four years, after which it will be sold as scrap for £100. The first allowance of 60 per cent is to be claimed in full.

It should be noted that the table assumes the plant was disposed of at the end of year 4, so that the scrap value of £100 came into that year's accounts. Also, if the scrap proceeds had been £200, so as to exceed the balance brought forward at £169 by £31, the company would have been required to include the £31 in its taxable profits of year 4 and suffer corporation tax accordingly.

It should be noted, too, that capital allowances are deductions from taxable profit, and *not* actual payments. This means that in cases where the company is making no profit, and hence is not liable for corporation tax, the company will receive no benefits from capital allowances unless they can be carried forward and deferred against profits at some future date.

Assuming that the company is profitable, and hence is paying corporation tax, the benefits from capital allowances will only accrue to the company when the corporation tax for that year is actually paid. Thus, if, in the above example, the company is profitable, and paying corporation tax at 40 per cent in one year in arrears, the actual (after tax) benefits to the project cash flow which result from the capital allowances are as shown in Table 3.3.

Table 3.3

				£
Year 1		600 x 0.4	=	£240
Year 2		100 x 0.4	=	40
Year 3		75 x 0.4	=	30
Year 4	(56 + 69 =)	125 x 0.4	=	50
Year 5				

PRE-TAX OR POST-TAX?

In chapters 1 and 2, where we dealt with the cash flows associated with capital investment projects and with methods of raising capital, we avoided discussion as to whether such cash flows should be calculated on a pre- or post-tax basis. In this chapter we have discussed the calculation of tax liability, but have again refrained from saying at what point notice should be taken of tax payments. The question is one that gives rise to argument and confusion in discussing techniques of capital investment appraisal. Before attempting to resolve the arguments and clarify the confusion it seems advisable to define precisely the two alternative procedures.

When the cash flows are calculated on a pre-tax basis, that cash flow which is associated with a given investment project in a given year is determined as follows. Estimate the profits of the company, before deduction of corporation tax, as they would be in that year if the project were not undertaken, and the profits, before corporation tax, as they would be if the project were undertaken. The difference between these two—the marginal contribution of the project to pre-tax profits—is the pre-tax cash flow associated with the project.

To calculate the post-tax cash flow associated with a given investment project in a given year, the procedure is identical to that just outlined, except that 'post-tax profits' are substituted for 'pre-tax profits' throughout. In other words, the post-tax cash flow is defined as the marginal contribution of the project to the profits of the company after deduction of corporation tax. The effects of taxation on the calculation of these post-tax flows are described below.

In the rest of this book we shall discuss different methods of evaluating project cash flows, but, except for certain types of company model described in chapter 8, the methods are equally applicable to pre- or post-tax cash flows. The decision as to which should be used depends on whether the objectives of the company are better defined as maximization of pre-tax profits or maximization of post-tax profits. Ultimately, most companies are (or should be) concerned with post-tax profits, and it is usually preferable therefore to evaluate capital projects on their post-tax cash flows. In addition, where the effect of capital allowances may be substantial, it is generally easier to work out the post-tax flows, as calculation of the pre-tax flows involves 'grossing up' these allowances. Ultimately, the decision will depend on convenience and how the company's objectives are stated.

- In many practical cases (particularly where substantial investment grants and capital allowances are not involved), the decisions will be the same whether pre- or post-tax flows are used, assuming that appropriate adjustments are made in the level of performance considered acceptable for a capital investment project.
- In those cases where the decision would be 'Accept' on the basis of pre-tax cash flows, and 'Reject' on the basis of post-tax flows (or vice versa), the tax position of the project is probably unusual. In this case, no general answer can be given as to which is right and which is wrong—the 'correct' answer can be determined only by careful evaluation of the reasons for the difference.

Pre-tax Cash Flows

The major part of the cash flows associated with a capital investment project consists of the capital expenditures, operating expenditures, and operating income. Since these are the same whether or not the company is actually going to pay corporation tax on its profits, they may be included directly in the pre-tax profits. A problem arises, however, when we examine the effects of capital allowances on the pre-tax cash flows: obviously they must be considered in any study of a capital investment project, and yet capital allowances cannot be claimed for the year under consideration if the company is not paying tax.

We first dispose of the case where the company is, either because of heavy losses, or very large tax-deductible expenses, not paying tax at all. Capital allowances can be ignored in that year since no allowances can be claimed against taxes which are not paid. They can in most cases be carried forward to offset against profits in following years (see p. 23).

Now consider the case where the company is paying corporation tax on its profits at, say, 40 per cent. Calculating capital allowances for the project as described above, suppose that the total allowances on the project we are considering in a particular year are £100; this means that £100 can be deducted from total profits before calculating corporation tax liability. In other words, the capital allowance is equivalent to a repayment by the government of the tax on £100—i.e., £40. So the *post*-tax profits are greater by £40 than they would have been had the allowances not been claimed. In order to equate this to pre-tax profits, we have to ask: What pre-tax profit would be equivalent to £40 after payment of corporation tax? Obviously the answer is

$$£40 \times \frac{100}{100 - 40} = £40 \times \frac{100}{60} = £66.7.$$

In other words, the post-tax payment must be 'grossed-up' by a factor of 100/60 in order to calculate the equivalent effect on pre-tax profits. This gives the correct figure to be included in the pre-tax cash flows of the project. (Included, of course, in the year in which the tax would have to be paid—typically one year after the actual capital expenditure takes place.) It should be noted that we have *not,* in the above discussions, considered two special cases: where the company is currently not paying tax, but expects to start paying tax in the next few years, and will carry forward its current losses and allowances to offset against future profits; or where the capital investment project under consideration could, if accepted, turn a tax-paying company into a non-tax-paying company, or vice versa. The analysis of such special cases, which arise particularly frequently in connection with mergers and take-overs, is beyond the scope of this book.

Post-tax Cash Flows

For the post-tax case, the calculations are usually more straightforward. First we calculate the actual pre-tax profits in each year, without considering capital allowances. Next, including tax allowances, as discussed above, we work out how much tax will be payable on the project cash flow associated with each year. This figure is then subtracted from the pre-tax cash flows in the year in which the tax is actually paid, typically one year later. These concepts are illustrated by showing how the after-tax cash flows are calculated for the case studies in chapters 1 and 2. In addition to the assumptions made there, we suppose that:

(a) The company is always making enough profit elsewhere to offset against tax any losses incurred in the project.
(b) Corporation tax is at 40 per cent, and is paid one year in arrears.
(c) All capital expenditure qualifies for a 60 per cent initial allowance, and a 25 per cent annual writing down allowance thereafter.
(d) None of the expenditure qualifies for an investment grant.

CASE STUDY: EXTENSION OF PRODUCT LINE

We shall now examine how these techniques are applied to calculate the post-tax cash flows for the case studies described in chapters 1 and 2. The first stage in the project for extension of product range, The first stage in a project for the extension of product, given the figures on p. 5, is to calculate the capital allowances in each year, following the procedure outlined on p. 23. For the £400 000 capital expenditure in year 0, the allowances will be £240 000 (60 per cent) in year 0, £40 000 (25 per cent of £160 000) in year 1, £30 000 (25 per cent of £120 000) in year 2, and so on. Similarly, for the £70 000 expenditure in year 1, the allowances will be £42 000 in year 1, £7000 in year 2, and so on. By the end of year 7, the written down value of the total expenditure will be £23 000, and there will therefore be a negative balancing allowance of £27 000 to

Table 3.4 *Extension of product range: effects of taxation (£'000s)*

Year	0	1	2	3	4	5	6	7	8	9
9. Capital allowances (as above)	240	82	37	28	21	16	12	10	–27	–
7. Net trading profit (from p. 5)	0	70	145	183	220	258	295	333	–	–
10. Profit for tax (7–9)	–240	–12	108	155	199	242	283	323	27	–
11. Tax at 40%, 1 year in arrears		–96	–5	43	62	80	97	113	129	11
8. Net cash flow (from p. 5)	–400	0	145	183	220	258	295	332	50	–
12. Post-tax cash flow	–400	96	150	140	148	178	198	219	–70	–11

Table 3.5 *Process control project: effects of taxation (£'000s)*

Year	0	1	2	3	4	5	6	7
8. Capital allowances	60	24	10	8	5	4	11	–
6. Net savings (from p. 6)	–	24	23	25	27	29	31	–
9. 'Profit' for tax (6–8)	–60	–	13	17	22	25	20	–
10. Tax at 40%, 1 year in arrears	–	–24	–	5	7	9	10	8
7. Net cash flow (from p. 6)	–100	4	23	25	27	29	31	–
11. Post tax cash flow (7–10)	–100	28	23	20	20	20	21	–8

Note: as there is no scrap value, the plant is written down to zero in year 6.

Table 3.6 *Alternative methods of finance: effects of taxation (£'000s)*

Method (a) 8% debenture issue

Year	0	1	2	3	4	5	6	7	8	9	10	11
1. Net cash flow (from p. 17)	5000	–400	–400	–400	–400	–400	–400	–400	–400	–400	–5400	–
2. Interest allowable against tax	–	–400	–400	–	–	–	–	–	–	–	–400	
3. Tax relief at 40%, 1 year in arrears	–	–	–	160	160	–	–	–	–	–	160	160
4. Post-tax cash	5000	–400	–240	–240	–	–	–	–	–	–	–5240	160

Method (b) Bank loan at 9%, repayable over 10 years

Year	0	1	2	3	4	5	6	7	8	9	10	11
1. Net cash flow (from p. 18)	5000	–950	–905	–860	–815	–770	–725	–680	–635	–590	–545	–
2. Interest allowable against tax	–	450	405	360	315	270	225	180	135	90	45	–
3. Tax relief at 40%, 1 year in arrears	–	–	180	162	144	126	108	90	72	54	36	18
4. Post-tax cash flow (1 + 3)	5000	–950	–725	–698	–671	–644	–617	–590	–563	–536	–511	18

Note: for *Method (c)*, the new equity issue, all cash flows on p. 18 are already post-tax.

'write up' the value to the £50 000 scrap value. Table 3.4 shows the detailed method of calculation of the post-tax cash flows for this project; Tables 3.5 and 3.6 show the corresponding calculations for the process control project, described on p.6, and for the alternative financing methods, described on pp. 17 and 18.

In chapter 1 we discussed the interface between the two stages of capital investment appraisal: producing forecasts of the way in which a project is expected to behave, and appraising the project on the basis of these forecasts. This interface—the output from stage one and the input to stage two—is the forecast set of cash flows associated with the project during its life. In the first three chapters of this book we have been concerned with stage one: the production of the forecast cash flows. From now on we shall be concerned with stage two: the appraisal of the projects, and we shall assume in discussing a project that the cash flows have been calculated already.

Checklist

1. Which taxes are likely to be of substantial relevance in making an investment decision?
2. Explain the difference between capital allowances and depreciation. How do they affect the cash flows associated with a project?
3. How would the cash flows in the examples on pp. 28 and 29 be modified under a continental tax system with tax levied at 50 per cent, payable in the year in which it is incurred?

4

General considerations: Payback: Rate of return

In chapters 1, 2, and 3 we defined capital investment projects and their associated cash flows, and discussed ways of raising capital for investment, and the ways in which taxation may affect the cash flows. In this chapter, and in subsequent chapters, we shall assume that the cash flows associated with the project or projects under consideration have been determined as accurately as possible; we shall be concerned with different ways of using that information to decide whether to accept or reject each capital investment project.

CLASSIFICATION OF INVESTMENT PROBLEMS

Given a set of possible investment projects, two important questions have to be answered before the correct decisions can be made:

(a) Are the forecast cash flows of the projects known with certainty, or are there potential sources of inaccuracy in them? In more practical terms, since there is always some degree of error inherent in making forecasts, how accurate are the forecasts and is it likely that errors in the forecasts could lead to a wrong decision?

(b) Can the decision to accept or reject any particular project be made independently of the decision to accept or reject any other project?

The answer to the first question in any practical case is likely to be that there is considerable uncertainty in forecasting at least some of the components of future cash flows. Typically, the initial capital expenditures can be determined with some accuracy (they are often based on prices quoted by suppliers or subcontractors), but the further into the future the cash flows are forecast, the more difficult it is to produce accurate forecasts. Nevertheless, forecasts of some kind have to be made if decisions are to be made at all, and an important part of any such forecasting procedure must be to estimate the magnitude of possible error in the forecasts produced.

The answer to the second question is likely to be similarly negative. Few companies have so much capital available that they can afford to undertake any investment project which looks attractive, irrespective of what other capital commitments have already been made elsewhere. This implies the necessity for some kind of capital rationing, and changes the investment problem from 'Is project X good enough?' to 'How should we allocate our resources of capital among the possible investment projects?'.

The possible combinations of answers to these groups of questions gives a convenient four-way classification of the basic capital investment appraisal problem. This classification is illustrated below.

		Forecasts	
		Certain	Uncertain
Decisions	Independent	A	B
	Interdependent	C	D

Most of the techniques currently in use for capital investment appraisal are satisfactory only for problems in class A—i.e., certain forecasts and independent decisions. The remainder of this chapter, together with chapters 5 and 6, will be devoted to describing and analysing these techniques. In chapter 7 we shall discuss techniques for dealing with risk and uncertainty (class B), while chapter 8 will cover problems in class C (certain but interdependent) and, in so far as any techniques exist, class D (uncertain and interdependent).

There is an apparent contradiction in the above paragraphs. Most real-life capital investment appraisal problems may be classified under class D, but most techniques that exist apply only to class A. Should we then conclude that the use of capital investment appraisal techniques such as those described in the rest of this book is pointless? The answer, of course, is 'No'. The fact that only a part of the total problem can be solved satisfactorily using analytical techniques is no justification for not using them. Moreover, by solving that part of the problem which can be dealt with satisfactorily, it is easier to isolate and define those parts which are dealt with less easily.

Despite the fact that analytical techniques seem only to solve a very special case of the general problem, we offer no apology for devoting the next two-and-a-half chapters to techniques for dealing with the problems of class A, and for completely ignoring, for the moment, problems of uncertain forecasts and interdependent decisions. In practice, the cash flows of many projects can be forecast with reasonable accuracy, and many projects (particularly those requiring relatively low capital expenditure) can be treated independently from other competing projects, even though this independence may not be complete. It is unquestionable that the systematic application even of techniques such as those described in chapters 5 and 6 can substantially improve the efficiency of the investment decision-making, and hence the long-term profitability of any company not already using such methods.

GENERAL CONSIDERATIONS

Before looking in detail at the different techniques used for capital investment appraisal, we should first consider what general criteria such techniques must satisfy. This will enable us to evaluate each technique according to certain defined criteria, and so to identify its advantages and disadvantages.

The object of any capital investment appraisal technique is to set up a decision rule for accepting or rejecting capital investment projects. We require, then, a rule which, given a set of possible capital investment projects, together with their associated cash flows, will produce the answer 'Accept' or 'Reject' for each project. Most decision rules for capital investment appraisal operate essentially in three stages:

(a) Reduce all available information about the project and its associated cash flows to one single number (payback period, rate of return, net present value, etc.).

(b) Compare that number with some given 'threshold' or 'cut-off' number.

(c) If the number associated with the project is better (shorter payback period, higher rate of return, higher net present value, etc.) than the threshold level, the project is accepted. If the number associated with the project is worse, the project is rejected.

A refinement is to add a fourth stage by providing the system with two threshold levels: a minimum, and a maximum. If the project is better than the maximum it is accepted automatically, if worse than the minimum, it is rejected. If the project falls between the two levels, the decision rule is regarded as failing to provide a clear indication as to whether the project should be accepted or rejected. This refinement is an extremely common—and useful—way of using a decision rule which is not entirely satisfactory; there may be occasions when a good case can be made for disagreeing with the results produced by a given decision rule. The rule can, however, be used to reduce the scope of the problem by eliminating those projects which are clearly 'good' or 'bad', and referring back for further study, more detailed evaluation of cash flows, etc., any project for which the decision rule is inadequate.

There are four basic conditions that a capital investment appraisal technique (and hence the corresponding decision rule) should satisfy:

- It should be unambiguous. If the same information can be interpreted using the same technique in more than one way, clear decisions obviously cannot be made.
- It should be consistent with intuitive ideas. In other words, it should not be possible to produce an example where the better decision is obviously A and the decision rule produces B. Specifically, it should be consistent with the two most obvious intuitive rules, which may be called 'the more the better' (i.e., other things being equal, a larger cash flow is preferred to a smaller one in the same time period) and 'the sooner the better' (i.e., other things being equal, a cash flow in an earlier time period is preferred to the same cash flow in a later period). If the technique does not produce sensible answers to questions where the answer from these rules is self-evident, then obviously little reliance can be placed on the answers produced in more complex cases where they are not self-evident.
- It should be widely applicable. For all the techniques in general use one can construct examples of projects for which either of the above conditions does not hold, or for which the decision rule is unsatisfactory for some other reason. A good decision rule should, however, be applicable to as many different projects as possible. Furthermore, it should be possible to identify in advance those projects for which the rule will not or may not be applicable.
- It should be easy to use. This does not necessarily imply that the calculations required have to be simple, since it is always possible to write computer programs to do the calculation. What is important is that the user (i.e., the decision-maker) should be able to understand what the use of a particular rule implies, and how he can evaluate the decision.

This book does not pretend to offer methods of appraising capital investment projects which completely satisfy all four conditions. There is, unfortunately, no method which is entirely satisfactory for all applications. In analysing and describing the different methods of capital investment appraisal, we shall try to assess the principal advantages and disadvantages of each technique, both from a logical examination of the assumptions implicit in using the technique and from practical experience.

Probably the simplest technique for capital investment appraisal is the 'payback' method, which depends on calculating a quantity known as the 'payback period' of a project. The payback period is defined simply as the length of time which elapses before the total capital expenditure of the project has been recouped. More formally, the payback period is the length of time which elapses between the beginning of the project and the point in time when the cumulative cash flow becomes positive. Thus, a project with initial capital expenditure of £1000 (in year 0), which earns an annual profit of £400 (starting in year 1), will have a payback period of 1000/400 = 2.5 years (see Table 4.1).

PAYBACK

Table 4.1 *Calculation of payback period*

Year	Cash flow (£)	Cumulative cash flow to date (£)
0	–1000	–1000
1	400	–600
2	400	–200
3	400	200
4	400	600

Payback period = $\frac{1000}{400}$ = 2.5 years

The payback period may be calculated for a variety of possible cash flows: pre- and post-tax, with or without the addition of depreciation to the cash flows, etc. Probably the most widely used method is to calculate the payback period for the pre-tax cash flow, as defined in the preceding chapters. The usual method of application of the payback period is for the company to have a 'cut-off' period, within which every capital investment project must have recouped its investment. The length of the cut-off period will depend on the precise definition of 'cash flows' and on the industry in which the company operates; a typical cut-off period for the engineering industry would be four years.

The comments about depreciation and tax in the preceding chapters apply equally to the determination of cash flow for payback: depreciation should be ignored in calculating cash flows, and the pre-/post tax decision is usually not of primary importance, provided that the cut-off period is determined accordingly (thus, a three-year payback for pre-tax cash flows would correspond roughly to a five-year payback for post-tax cash flows). The following discussion of the advantages and disadvantages of this method apply for any variant.

In addition to being one of the simplest methods, payback is one of the most widely used. Surveys in the UK and USA have shown that in each country a substantial majority of companies uses some form of payback as its primary method of capital investment appraisal. (Payback is also the primary, if not the only, method of appraisal used in communist countries, where the use of any concepts involving interest or discounting may generate ideological complications.) Against this, modern textbooks on finance are almost universal in their condemnation of payback methods as leading to bad decision-making. In order to analyse the reasons for this apparent conflict we shall analyse the technique to see how far it satisfies each of the four requirements laid down for our 'ideal' capital investment appraisal technique.

First, the technique should be unambiguous. Unfortunately, payback is not entirely satisfactory on this count. Table 4.2 shows an example similar to that in Table 4.1, except that the project requires an additional expenditure of £700 in year 4. It is easy to see that the cumulative cash flow becomes positive in year 3, then negative again in year 4, and finally positive once more in year 5. According as to whether we take the first or second 'payback', so we get a payback period of either 2.50 years or 4.25 years. Obviously this leads to difficulties: if we try to compare this project with a given 'cut-off level' of 3.00 years, the project either could be accepted or rejected, depending on which payback period is used.

Table 4.2

Year	Cash flow (£)	Cumulative cash flow (£)
0	–1000	–1000
1	400	–600
2	400	–200
3	400	200
4	–300	–100
5	400	300
6	400	700

1st payback period = 2.50 years
2nd payback period = 4.25 years

For many projects this difficulty will not arise. In particular, in any project involving only one capital expense at the beginning and thereafter always showing a profit, the cumulative cash flow will always increase, and hence once it has turned positive it can never become negative again. However, since projects frequently do arise which require additional injection of capital after the start, or where for some reason the cash flow may go negative, this ambiguity is a serious problem. It is of course always possible to remove the ambiguity by defining the payback period as the first (or the last) of the possible payback periods; but this is arbitrary and hence unsatisfactory.

Secondly, the technique should be consistent with intuition. Here again there are disadvantages with payback. Although very often projects with a short payback period appear on intuitive grounds to be better than those with longer payback periods, it is very easy to construct examples which contradict intuitive ideas.

In (a) in Table 4.3, the cash flows are given for two projects: A and B. Each project requires £1000 capital outlay in year 0 and has an operating life of six years. Project A generates £400 profit per year over the six year period, while project B shows a steady increase from £200 profit in year 1 to £1200 profit in year 6. As the cumulative cash flow figures show, project A has a payback period of 2.5 years and project B a payback period of 2.7 years. Nevertheless, since the cash flows associated with project B in years 3 to 6 are so much better than those of project A in that period, any manager would prefer project B to project A—even though he has to wait a little longer to see his capital repaid.

Example (b) in Table 4.3 is another case where payback does not provide a decision consistent with intuition. The same project

Table 4.3

(a)	*Project A*		*Project B*	
Year	Cash flow (£)	Cumulative cash flow (£)	Cash flow (£)	Cumulative cash flow (£)
0	–1000	–1000	–1000	–1000
1	400	–600	200	–800
2	400	–200	400	–400
3	400	200	600	–200
4	400	600	800	1000
5	400	1000	1000	2000
6	400	1400	1200	3200
	Payback period = 2.5 years		Payback period = 2.7 years	

(b)	*Project A*		*Project C*	
Year	Cash flow (£)	Cumulative cash flow (£)	Cash flow (£)	Cumulative cash flow (£)
0	–1000	–1000	–1000	–1000
1	400	–600	500	–400
2	400	–200	300	–200
3	400	200	400	200
4	400	600	400	600
5	400	1000	400	1000
6	400	1400	400	1400
	Payback period = 2.5 years		Payback period = 2.5 years	

A is now compared with project C, which differs from project A only in that its cash flow is £100 greater in year 1 and £100 less in year 2. Both projects have the same payback period (2.5 years), but project C is clearly preferable to project A because some of the capital is repaid sooner.

These two examples illustrate the two most serious shortcomings of the payback method: it takes no account of the cash flows after the end of the payback period, and it takes no account of the so-called 'time value' of money (i.e., other things being equal, £1 today is always preferable to £1 next year, if only because £1 today may be invested to produce more than £1 next year). It has been suggested that these two disadvantages, given the very wide use of payback in the UK and USA, have been a major hindrance in the development of good long-range planning systems in these two countries.

Thirdly, the technique should be widely applicable. Despite the examples given in Tables 4.2 and 4.3, it is obvious that many types of projects will occur where the cash flows are not such that they lead to difficulties of these kinds. Unfortunately, since there is no simple method of knowing in advance whether such difficulties will arise, the method cannot be recommended for general use. A single exception may be the case where all the potential projects to be considered by a company have very similar cash flow patterns. Under these circumstances, it is probable that the use of a payback criterion would generally lead to the correct decisions. In such an ideal case, however, it is only fair to point out than any sensible criterion would lead to the same results; hence there are no particular grounds for preferring payback even here.

Finally, the technique should be easy to use. Here, of course, lies the major advantage of payback. The concept is simple to understand, and the necessary calculations are easy to perform. Even so, the disadvantages of payback outlined above are in the opinion of the author so great as to override this consideration. We shall see in chapter 5 that the 'sophisticated' techniques based on discounted cash flow methods overcome most of the disadvantages of payback and are, in reality, not much more complex to calculate.

RATE OF RETURN

Another technique which is widely used and relatively simple to calculate is the use of the 'accounting rate of return', sometimes called the 'average rate of return' or simply the 'rate of return'. As with payback, a number of variations of this method exist. Depreciation may or may not be included in the cash flows, and the cash flows may be calculated on a pre- or post-tax basis. The most common method is to use the operating cash flows on a pre-tax basis—but after the deduction of depreciation. The general comments and discussion which follow will apply, with only marginal changes, to other methods of calculation.

The basic concept behind the calculation of rate of return is inherent in the question: At what interest rate would the same amount of capital have to be invested in order to produce the same total income over the life of the project?

The rate of return is calculated in three stages:

(a) Determine the average income per year (e.g., operating cash flow after depreciation but before tax) obtained from the project over its useful life. Note that only *operating revenue* and expenditure are included, not capital expenditure—the idea is to compare operating income against capital expended, and it is therefore necessary to separate the two completely.

(b) Determine the total capital invested on the project. Two alternative definitions are possible: either the total capital laid out at the start of the project (method 1), or the average value of the capital asset over the life of the project, after allowing for depreciation (method 2).

(c) The average income per year divided by the capital invested gives the rate of return.

Table 4.4 illustrates this calculation in a practical example. The project is that described as 'project A' in Table 4.3, with the further information that the entire £1000 expenditure in year 0 is for the purchase of a capital asset, which is then depreciated at £150 per year for six years, the residual value of £100 being written off in the final year of the project.

In order to convert the cash flows given in Table 4.3 into average income, we have first to remove the capital expense figure (£1000 in year 0), and then correct for depreciation. Adding up the 'income' column and dividing by 6 gives the average income: £233 per year. Using method 1, we divide this by the total capital expended to get a rate of return of

$$\frac{233}{1000} = 23.3\%$$

Using method 2, we have first to calculate the average capital invested. Since the initial value is £1000, and the asset is depreciated by £150 per year for six years, leaving a final residual value of £100,

Table 4.4 *Calculation of rate of return*

Year	Operating cash flow (£)	Depreciation (£)	Profit (operating cash flow after depreciation) (£)
1	400	150	250
2	400	150	250
3	400	150	250
4	400	150	250
5	400	150	250
6	400	250	150

Total cash flow after depreciation (excluding initial capital expenditure)	= £1400
Average cash flow per year after depreciation	$= £\frac{1400}{6} = 233$
Rate of return (method 1)	$= \frac{233}{1000} =$ 23.3 per cent
Average value of depreciated asset	= £550
Rate of return (method 2)	$= \frac{233}{550} =$ 42.4 per cent

the average value is £550. Hence, the rate of return as determined by method 2 is

$$\frac{233}{550} = 42.4\%$$

In order to evaluate the worth of the rate of return method, we shall again measure it against each of the four criteria defined above.

- It should be unambiguous. In general the rate of return method is satisfactory on this count. The only qualification is that, by using method 2, the definition of 'average capital invested' may need some clarification when several different capital expenditures are involved at different times during the project.
- It should be consistent with intuition. Unfortunately, as in the case of the payback technique, it is all too easy to construct examples where the use of rate of return would either fail to lead to a decision, or lead to an obviously wrong decision. Consider the example in Table 4.5, where project A is taken from Table 4.3, while projects B and C have rather different patterns of profit. The capital expenditure and depreciation are the same in all three cases. Using the methods of calculation described above it can be seen that, whether method 1 or method 2 is used, all three projects have the same rate of return;

but they are obviously not equally attractive. Because project B produces its profit substantially earlier than project A, while project C produces its profit substantially later than project A, it is clear that in practice B would be preferred to A, and A to C. As with payback, the rate of return technique takes no account of the 'time value of money' and hence will fail to distinguish between these projects. A slight modification of the

Table 4.5 *Profit (operating cash flow after depreciation)*

Year	Project	A	B	C
1		250	400	100
2		250	300	150
3		250	250	200
4		250	200	250
5		250	150	300
6		150	100	400
Rate of return (method 1)		23.3%	23.3%	23.3%
Rate of return (method 2)		42.4%	42.4%	42.4%

example could actually lead to the *wrong* decision being made when a rate of return criterion is used. A further disadvantage is found in the use of depreciation when calculating the operating income, since changing the depreciation rate will alter the rate of return for the project. Since depreciation is an internal accounting convention and does not represent an actual cash flow, this is obviously unsatisfactory, and inconsistent with intuitive ideas.

- It should be widely applicable. The disadvantages spelled out in the previous example seriously limit the applicability of rate of return as a useful technique for capital investment appraisal.
- It should be easy to use. Even in this respect, rate of return lacks the advantages of payback. It may be necessary to involve depreciation and hence decide which rates of depreciation are appropriate; also the user must decide whether method 1 or method 2 is preferable.

The discussion in the previous paragraphs emphasizes that both payback and rate of return, the two most widely used 'conventional' methods of appraisal, have sufficiently severe disadvantages to render them of very little use. Both methods have a common feature, responsible for many of their shortcomings, in that they are based on concepts derived from financial accounting. Thus, payback is really a measure of liquidity rather than profitability, while rate of return is based on the concept of return on capital employed rather than return on future capital to be invested. In chapters 5 and 6 we shall investigate methods based on concepts derived from economic principles, which are in general much more satisfactory for evaluating capital investment projects.

Checklist

1. Explain what is meant by 'dependent/independent projects', and by 'certain/uncertain forecasts'. Into which of the corresponding categories do most capital investment problems fall? What are the advantages and disadvantages of assuming that a project is independent, and that you can make certain forecasts?
2. Summarize the four criteria that a technique for capital investment appraisal should satisfy. How important do you think each of these criteria is?
3. What are the principal advantages and disadvantages of payback? Find a real-life example where the use of one of these techniques has led to a bad decision.

5
Net present value

In this chapter we discuss the concept of the 'time value' of money, and introduce the basic idea of discounting as a method of taking account of the time value. The 'net present value method' is described, as well as its use for capital investment appraisal. A case study illustrates its application to lease/buy decisions.

TIME VALUE OF MONEY

In chapter 4, we referred several times to the so-called 'time-value' of money. In its simplest form, this is the choice between being given £1 in cash today, and a promissory note to pay £1 in cash one year hence. You would obviously prefer to take £1 now, even should you be certain that the promissory note will be paid. Why? . . . You can invest the £1 today for a period of one year, and one year from today you will have—not only the original £1—but the interest earned on that £1 during the intervening year. The 'time-value' of money is, of course, a more precise version of the concept referred to in chapter 4 as 'the sooner-the-better' rule.

In the case of a company contemplating a list of possible capital investment projects, there are obviously strong reasons for accepting (other things being equal) those projects which produce a positive cash flow as soon as possible. Not only may such funds be invested, as in the simple example above, but they may also be used to enable loans to be repaid earlier than would otherwise have been the case, saving financial charges, and possibly enabling other captial investment projects to be undertaken sooner.

These facts are obvious, and the manager operating purely instinctively will try to select those projects which produce positive cash flows as soon as possible. In some cases (like some of the examples in chapter 4) the choice is easy: one project clearly produces more income before others, and hence is preferable. In other cases the problem becomes more complex: while it is obvious that £1 today is preferable to £1 one year from today, it is open to question whether £10 today is always preferable to £11 next year, or £10 today to £17 five years from now.

To answer this type of question, and to develop procedures for dealing with general problems of capital investment appraisal which take account of the time value of money, we need to introduce the concept of discounted cash flow. This concept, and various techniques of appraisal based on it, will occupy the remainder of this chapter and chapter 6.

DISCOUNTED CASH FLOW

Discounted cash flow (DCF) is the generic name for a set of techniques and procedures based on a method for reducing cash flows which take place at different times to a common basis—thus enabling comparisons between them to be made.

The method, in its simplest form, assumes that the potential investor is operating in a perfect capital market. In other words, he can always borrow sums of money of any size at a specific fixed rate of interest, and can always invest any surplus money, obtaining on his investment the same interest rate that he has to pay for borrowed money. Let us suppose that this interest rate, usually called the 'discount rate', is fixed at 10 per cent: £1 invested today at 10 per cent will be worth £1.1 one year hence; this sum in the second year will earn interest of 10 per cent, and at the end of the second year will be worth £1.1 x (1 + 0.1) = £1.21. This compounding continues for years 3, 4, and so on. In general, for an interest rate i, £1 invested today will be worth £$(1 + i)$ one year from now, £$(1 + i)^2$ two years from now, and so on. This basic compounding rule gives us the fundamental equation of DCF:

$$\text{£1 today (year 0)} = \text{£}(1 + i)^n \text{ in } n \text{ years' time (year } n\text{)}.$$

Assuming again a 10 per cent discount rate, we also need to be able to anwer the question: If £1 today is worth £1.1 in one year's time, then what is the worth today of £1 in one year's time? Obviously, the answer is £1/1.1 = £0.909. Similarly, £1 in two years' time is equivalent today to £$1/(1.1)^2$ = £0.826, and so on.

For the general case, with interest rate i, we have an equation which corresponds exactly to the equation for compounding above:

$$\text{£1 in year } n = \text{£} \frac{1}{(1 + i)^n} \text{ in year 0.}$$

This 'correction factor' $1/(1 + i)^n$ by which £1 in year n must be multiplied to give the equivalent value in year 0, is known as the 'discount factor'. (In this discussion, and throughout this book, it has been assumed that sufficient accuracy is achieved by looking at cash flows in one-year periods. This effectively assumes that all cash flows during a year take place on the last day of that year—an assumption which will not lead to substantial inaccuracies for projects with a life of at least four to five years. Where the project life is less than this, and where the cost of capital is very high (say over 15 per cent) inaccuracies may arise. To overcome these discrepancies, more refined versions of DCF may be used which take account of shorter time periods; the discussion of such techniques is however beyond the scope of this book.)

We are now equipped with the general formula for comparing different cash flows at different periods in time, and, if we again assume a 10 per cent discount rate, we are in a position to answer specific questions of the kind posed above.

Is £10 today preferable to £11 next year? Applying the formula

$$\text{£11 in year 1} = \text{£11} \times \frac{1}{1.1} = \text{£10 in year 0.}$$

Hence, at a 10 per cent discount rate, £11 next year is worth exactly the same as £10 today.

Is £10 today preferable to £17 in 5 years' time? Again applying the formula

$$\text{£17 in 5 years} = \text{£17} \times \frac{1}{(1.1)^5} = \text{£17} \times \frac{1}{1.611} = \text{£17} \times 0.621 = \text{£10.57 in year 0.}$$

Hence, £17 in five years' time is equivalent to £10.57 today, and so is preferable to the alternative of £10 today.

In both these cases, we have answered the question by equating the future cash flow to an equivalent cash flow today. Obviously, the same question would have been answered by asking 'To what is £10 today equivalent in one year's time?' (£11) and 'To what is £10 today equivalent in five years' time?' ($\text{£10} \times (1.1)^5 = \text{£10} \times 1.611 = \text{£16.11}$). Although the two procedures will of course always give the same answer, it is usually more convenient to equate all cash flows to those in year 0 (today). This process of 'bringing back' cash flows to their equivalent values today is called 'discounting', and the equivalent value today is called the 'present value' of the cash flow.

Before discussing the general applications of this procedure, and introducing the 'net present value' method, we examine in rather more detail the implications of the perfect capital market assumption, and how a discount rate should be chosen.

Choice of a Discount Rate

In the previous section, we stated that the DCF method relies on the assumption that the potential investor may always borrow any sum of money at a fixed interest rate, and that he may always invest surplus capital at the same interest rate. In practice this situation is of course never realized; there are limits on how much may be borrowed or invested at a given rate, and the rates of interest for borrowing and investing are never the same. Two questions therefore arise: What discount rate should be used? Is the real-life situation so far from the theoretical ideal of a perfect capital market to render the concept of discounting at a single rate of little use?

Basically, there are two possible situations for a company with regard to its capital investments: either it has limited capital resources, and may have to reject otherwise attractive projects because of lack of capital, or it has, or can raise, all the capital that is required for implementing any capital investment project. We shall say that a company is 'capital constrained' or 'not capital constrained' according as to whether or not it finds itself in the first or second situation.

If a company is not capital constrained, its principal source of extra capital is usually from loans. The main consideration therefore in determining the discount rate is that the earlier the cash flows are received the sooner its outstanding loans can be repaid, and hence the less interest will be paid. Thus, if £10 is received in year 0 instead of in year 1, the company saves one year's interest—£1 if the interest rate is 10 per cent. In other words, £10 in year 0 can be considered equivalent to £11 in year 1. Obviously, then, 10 per cent (the interest rate on the loan) is the correct discount rate to use. If the extra capital is from some other source (retained earnings or new equity issues), then the figure to be used for the discount rate is the 'cost of capital'—a figure which represents the equivalent interest rate which would be paid if the capital were borrowed. This 'cost of capital' will be discussed in more detail in chapter 6.

When a company is capital constrained, its considerations must be rather different. If a decision is made to allocate capital to one particular project, the decision may result in some other project being deprived of capital. Thus the relevant question is not 'How much does the capital cost?' but rather 'What rate of return would be obtained on the capital if it were invested elsewhere?'. In other words: What is the 'opportunity cost' associated with the capital?

To illustrate this consideration, suppose there is available as an alternative project an investment which earns a steady 20 per cent per year (i.e., an investment of £10 in the project in year 0 produces an income of £2 in each succeeding year). An investment of this £10 in some other project would preclude the investment of the sum in this first project, and hence the investor would forfeit his £2 per year return. This can be regarded as 'borrowing' the capital from the first project in order to allocate it elsewhere. The appropriate discount rate is therefore the cost of 'borrowing' the capital from the alternative project (i.e., 20 per cent). In the case where a company is capital constrained, therefore, the discount rate which should be used is the rate of return which would have been obtained on the alternative project. (Note that the discussion here avoids the question of the correct definition of 'rate of return'. Strictly this should be the *internal* rate of return, which will be defined in chapter 6.) In practice, the situation is rarely so simple as a straight choice between two projects, and the above statements need some modification. Usually, in the capital constrained case, the most practical procedure is to take as the discount rate the average rate of return obtained historically by the company on all capital projects.

We are now in a position to examine the implications of the 'perfect capital market' assumptions made above. If the rates of interest actually paid on different loans (or more generally the costs of different parts of the capital) vary substantially, then the choice of a single discount rate in a non-constrained situation may prove difficult. However, as we are in practice concerned only with the marginal capital requirements for a particular capital investment project, and not with the whole capital structure of the company, the rate of interest of marginal capital may be used. In other words, the appropriate discount rate to be used is the cost of borrowing the additional capital required from the project.

Conversely, if in a constrained case the rates of interest obtainable on different projects vary substantially, the calculation of a single average rate may conceal other relevant information. Where capital availability is constrained, the pre-condition of independent decisions is violated (since giving the money to one project necessarily implies taking it away from another). Where these independencies become significant, the only entirely satisfactory way is to use more general models of the type described in chapter 8.

There remains the assumption that the borrowing rate and the investing rate are equal. As long as the company avoids becoming capital constrained, the above arguments indicate that it needs only to consider the borrowing rate; and thus the fact that the investing rate is different is unimportant. Similarly, where the company is always capital constrained, only the investing rate is relevant. Thus, the only case where this assumption may lead to difficulties is where the company is sometimes capital constrained and sometimes not. More general discounted cash flow methods based on two different rates of return are available for this type of problem.

NET PRESENT VALUE

We have defined a method for determining equivalent values for cash flows at different points in time by bringing them to a common basis. The simplest and most widely used discounted cash flow method for capital investment consists essentially of calculating the values in year 0 (the 'present') of all the cash flows associated with the project, and then adding these values together. The resultant total is called the 'net present value' (NPV) of the project (also known as the 'present value', and the 'discounted present value').

If the NPV is greater than zero, the return from the project will more than cover the cost of the capital, and the project should therefore be accepted. If the NPV is less than zero, the project is rejected.

Table 5.1 illustrates the application of this method to the cash flows for projects A, B, and C, used as examples in Table 4.3. The

Table 5.1 *Net present value calculations for three projects*

Year	Cash flow (£)	Discount factor at 10%	Value in year 0 (£)	Discount factor at 15%	Value in year 0 (£)
			Project A		
0	−1000	1	−1000 x 1 = −1000.0	1.0	−1000
1	400	1/1.1 = 0.909	400 x 0.909 = 364	0.870	348
2	400	$1/(1.1)^2$ = 0.826	400 x 0.826 = 330	0.756	322
3	400	$1/(1.1)^3$ = 0.751	400 x 0.751 = 300	0.658	263
4	400	$1/(1.1)^4$ = 0.683	400 x 0.683 = 273	0.572	229
5	400	$1/(1.1)^5$ = 0.621	400 x 0.621 = 248	0.497	199
6	400	$1/(1.1)^6$ = 0.565	400 x 0.564 = 226	0.432	173
	Net present value of project: at 10% =		£741	at 15% =	£534
			Project B		
0	−1000	1	−1000 x 1 = −1000.0	1.0	−1000
1	200	0.909	200 x 0.909 = 182	0.870	174
2	400	0.826	400 x 0.826 = 340	0.756	322
3	600	0.751	600 x 0.751 = 451	0.658	395
4	800	0.683	800 x 0.683 = 546	0.572	458
5	1000	0.621	1000 x 0.621 = 621	0.497	497
6	1200	0.565	1200 x 0.564 = 673	0.432	519
	Net present value of project: at 10% =		£1838	at 15% =	£1365
			Project C		
0	−1000	1	−1000 x 1 = −1000.0	1.0	−1000
1	500	0.909	500 x 0.909 = 455	0.870	396
2	300	0.826	300 x 0.826 = 248	0.756	227
3	400	0.751	400 x 0.751 = 300	0.658	263
4	400	0.683	400 x 0.683 = 273	0.572	229
5	400	0.621	400 x 0.621 = 248	0.497	199
6	400	0.565	400 x 0.564 = 226	0.432	173
	Net present value of project: at 10% =		£750	at 15% =	£487

first column gives the net cash flow of the project in each year of operation, the second contains the discount factor, calculated from the expression $1/(1 + i)^n$, while the third column, obtained by multiplying the first two columns, gives the equivalent value in year 0 of the cash flow in each year. The sum of this last column is of course the net present value of the entire sequence of cash flows, and therefore the NPV of the project.

Some textbooks prefer to define the net present value of projects as the NPV of all operating cash flows, excluding the initial capital expenditure. Using the same discount rate of 10 per cent this would give NPVs of projects A, B, and C, as £1741.6, £1837.0, and £1749.0, respectively. The NPV of the operating cash flow is then compared with the initial capital outlay, and the project is considered desirable if the NPV is greater than the initial capital. This implies that the rate of return obtained on the project is greater than the discount rate used for the cost of the capital (the actual cost in the non-capital case or the opportunity cost in the capital constrained case). Hence, the project is profitable.

More formally, if the initial capital outlay in year 0 is I, the operating income in years 0, 1, 2, etc. is $I_0, I_1, I_2, \ldots I_n$ respectively, and the discount rate is i, then the project is considered desirable if:

$$I < I_0 \frac{I_1}{1+i} + \frac{I_2}{(1+i)^2} + \cdots \frac{I_n}{(1+i)^n} = \sum_{r=0}^{n} \frac{I_r}{(1+i)^r}. \qquad (1)$$

This compares with our original definition of NPV, where the capital expenditure is included in the cash flow, and the NPV of the project is defined as the NPV of *all* cash flows associated with it. Formally, if C_i is the cash flow in year i, we have:

$$C_0 = I + I_0, C_1 = I_1, C_2 = I_2, \cdots$$

$$\text{NPV} = C_0 + \frac{C_1}{(1+i)} + \frac{C_2}{(1+i)^2} + \cdots = \sum_{r=0}^{n} \frac{C_r}{(1+i)^r}. \qquad (2)$$

Using this definition, the criterion for desirability is that the net present value of the project should be positive (i.e., is greater than zero). As in the preceding case, this implies that the return obtained on the project is greater than the cost of the capital invested in it and hence the company will be better off overall by implementing the project. More generally, of course, the greater the NPV of a project the more desirable it is, and, given a choice between two projects, the project with higher NPV will be selected.

The advantage of including the capital expenditure as part of the cash flows in the NPV is that it takes care automatically of cases where the initial capital expenditure occurs over several years, as well as those where distinct capital expenditures exist at different points in the life of the project. Such cases raise difficulties in the alternative definition we have mentioned, which do not arise with the first.

In chapter 4, we laid down four criteria which our capital investment appraisal technique should satisfy. In concluding this section, we shall examine how NPV measures up to these criteria.

- It should be unambiguous. Here our definition of NPV is quite satisfactory; as long as the discount rate is given, the method of calculation will always give exactly one NPV for a given project.
- It should be consistent with intuition. Here again NPV comes out well. It takes account of all the cash flows associated with a project during its entire lifetime, and also allows for the time value of money; NPV resolves quite easily the questions posed in Table 4.3 which show up the weaknesses of payback. The calculations of NPV in Table 5.2, show that project B is substantially better than project A, while project C is marginally better than project A. Both conclusions are consistent with intuition.
- It should be widely applicable. The discussion on pp. 45–47 indicates the major weakness of NPV. It may be difficult to determine a suitable discount rate and, where a company is sometimes capital constrained and sometimes not, there may be conceptual problems about using the method at all. (These problems can be resolved by using the internal rate of return in the first case, and NPV using two discount rates in the second. Both methods are described in chapter 6.) However, as long as the problem of determining the discount rate does not arise, the method may always be used. When the investor is big (e.g., an international corporation, or a government) the non-constrained assumption virtually always holds, and the method can be used without qualification.
- It should be easy to use. One of the principal objections to using DCF methods in general is that they are difficult to understand and need a lot of calculation. This, in our opinion, is not true. Once the basic idea that £1 this year is worth more than £1 next year is understood, the calculation of NPV, too, may be readily understood. With a set of discount factor tables (see Appendix) and a desk calculator, the process of 'converting' from cash flow to NPV can be done in a matter of minutes. It is true that in some cases the calculation of the cash flows may be rather complex, but this problem may exist with any analysis of capital projects. In any event, decision-making,

particularly taking decisions with long-term effects such as those concerned with capital projects, is not a good area for economizing, and the few man-hours or man-days necessary to produce good decisions constitutes one of the best investments a company can make.

Note In the examples given in Table 5.1, we have calculated the discount factor using the formula stated on p. 44. In practice this is unnecessary, as comprehensive tables exist, giving the values of discount factors for different discount rates. The appendix contains such a table, and gives discount factors for discount rates from 1 to 40 per cent for time periods from 1 to 40 years. Use of such tables will, of course, greatly facilitate NPV calculations.

Case Study: Lease or Buy

As an example of how NPV can be applied, we now look at a case study of one of the most common of all capital investment decision problems. Given that a company needs a particular capital asset, should it lease the asset or buy it outright?

The PQR Company has decided it needs a new computer system. The system will, if purchased outright, cost £1 million in year 0. The probable life is five years, starting at the end of year 0, and its estimated resale value at the end of five years is £100 000. The computer manufacturer has offered a rental contract for years 1–5 inclusively at an annual cost of £250 000. If bought, the computer would qualify for a 20 per cent investment grant, and capital allowances of 60 per cent in year 1 and a reducing balance of 25 per cent thereafter. Corporation tax is assumed to be at 40 per cent, payable one year in arrears, and the company is sufficiently profitable to be able to offset all the computer costs against tax.

The company has the capital available, but may require it for an alternative project. This alternative project is expected to earn between 10 and 15 per cent after tax.

First, note that the decision to obtain a new computer has been made already. Hence, it is not necessary to evaluate the benefits to be generated by the project—it will be sufficient to compare the NPVs of the two cost cash flows and select the option which gives the better (lower) NPV. Table 5.2 sets out the details of the calculations.

At a discount rate of 10 per cent, alternative B is just preferable (£603 000 compared with £610 000), while at a 15 per cent discount rate the alternative B is substantially better (£548 000 compared with £613 000). Note that the NPV of alternative B is much more sensitive to the choice of discount rate than is the

Table 5.2 *Lease or buy: NPV calculations (£'000s)*

Year	0	1	2	3	4	5	6	7	
Alternative A: Buy									
1. Capital expenditure	1000	–	–	–	–	–	–100	–	
2. Less investment grant	200	–	–	–	–	–	–	–	
3. Net capital expenditure (1–2)	800	–	–	–	–	–	–100	–	
4. Capital allowances	480	80	60	45	34	26	5	–	
5. Tax allowed		192	32	24	18	14	10	2	
6. Net cash flow *out* (3–5)	800	–192	–32	–24	–18	–14	90	–2	
									Total
NPV at 10% discount rate	800	–174	–27	–18	–12	–9	51	–1	610
NPV at 15% discount rate	800	–167	–25	–16	–10	–7	39	–1	613
Alternative B: Lease									
1. Leasing costs	–	250	250	250	250	250	–	–	
2. Tax allowed	–	–	100	100	100	100	100	–	
3. Net cash flow *out* (3–5)	–	250	150	150	150	150	–100	–	
									Total
NPV at 10% discount rate	–	227	124	113	102	93	–56		603
NPV at 15% discount rate	–	218	113	99	86	75	–43		548

NPV of alternative A; this is intuitively understandable as the bulk of A's cash flow is in year 0, while B's is spread out over the life of the project.

Checklist

1. What is the underlying principle of DCF methods? How realistic are the assumptions on which the method depends?
2. What are the main advantages of DCF methods over non-DCF methods?
3. What would you consider an appropriate discount rate to use in NPV calculations for:
   (a) Evaluating an inter-city motorway?
   (b) Evaluating personal investment decisions?
   (c) Evaluating capital projects within your company?
4. Could the NPV method be used for evaluating take-overs? What would be the appropriate discount rate in this case?

6
Other DCF methods

The net present value method described in chapter 5 represents a substantial improvement over the non-DCF methods described in chapter 4. However, there are still several problems, which principally concern the assumption of a perfect capital market. In this chapter we discuss several other DCF methods which attempt to evade or overcome these problems. These techniques are compared critically with the NPV method.

INTERNAL RATE OF RETURN

In chapter 5, we noted that the principal conceptual difficulties inherent in using NPV are associated with the problem of choosing a discount rate. One technique which solves this particular problem (by neatly evading the issue) is the use of the 'internal rate of return' method—also known variously as 'yield', 'discounted cash flow rate of return', 'project rate of return', 'time-adjusted rate of return', or simply 'rate of return'.

The internal rate of return derives from the equation given on p. 48 to define net present value:

$$\text{NPV} = C_0 + \frac{C_1}{1+i} + \frac{C_2}{(1+i)^2} + \cdots = \sum_{r=0}^{n} \frac{C_r}{(1+i)^r}$$

where i is the discount rate and C_r the cash flow in year r. The appropriate decision rule is that if the NPV is greater than zero the project should be accepted; if the NPV less than zero the project should be rejected.

With this in mind, we can reverse the question 'What is the NPV if the discount rate is i?' and ask instead 'What discount rate gives zero NPV?' This discount rate is called the 'internal rate of return' (IRR).

The IRR may equivalently be defined as that discount rate which makes the NPV of all negative cash flows equal to the NPV of all positive cash flows. In the simplest type of project, where an initial capital outlay gives negative cash flow in year 0, and revenues from the project give positive cash flows in all subsequent years, the IRR may also be defined as the discount rate which makes the NPV of the revenues exactly equal to the initial capital outlay.

Whichever definition is used, the basic idea is the same: the IRR represents, in some sense, the rate of return on capital expended which the company would obtain by investing in the project. To see this more explicitly we will look at a simple example. Consider a project with initial capital outlay of £100, and income of £60 and £55 in years 1 and 2 respectively. Then the NPV of the project at discount rate i is given by:

$$\text{NPV} = -100 + \frac{60}{1+i} + \frac{55}{(1+i)^2}$$

and the IRR is the value of i which satisfies the equation

$$0 = -100 + \frac{60}{1+i} + \frac{55}{(1+i)^2}.$$

By trying $i = 0.1$, we see that this value satisfies the equation. Hence, the IRR of this project is 0.1 or 10 per cent.

Ten per cent can also be regarded as the rate of interest paid by the project (or earned by the company). From this point of view, each of the two positive cash flows can be regarded in part as payments of interest and in part as repayments of the initial capital:

Year 1: interest on £100 for 1 year at 10% = £10
hence 'repayment' of capital = £60 – 10 = £50
hence capital outstanding = £100 – £50 = £50.

Year 2: interest on £50 for 1 year at 10% = £5
hence 'repayment' of capital = £55 – 5 = £50
hence capital outstanding = £50 – 50 = £0.

The IRR, then, is that interest rate which results in the capital outlay being just paid off by the incoming cash flows at the end of the life of the project, after deduction of 'interest payments' for capital outstanding.

In practice, of course, the value of the IRR will not always be obvious by inspection, as it was in the preceding example. In most cases the IRR is best calculated by evaluating the NPV for several distinct discount rates, and then determining the discount rate corresponding to zero NPV by graphical interpolation (alternatively, a simple computer program can be used to perform the calculation). This method is illustrated in Table 6.1 and Fig. 6.1.

In order to use the IRR for decision-making, we need only note that (subject to certain conditions being satisfied) the NPV is a decreasing function of the IRR. In other words, the greater the IRR the smaller the NPV, and vice versa. Thus, if the discount rate is

Table 6.1 *NPV at different interest rates (£)*

Year	Cash flow	Discounted cash flows at 0%	5%	10%
0	–1000	–1000	–1000	–1000
1	100	100	95.2	90.9
2	150	150	136.0	123.9
3	200	200	172.8	150.2
4	250	250	205.7	170.7
5	300	300	235.2	186.3
6	350	350	261.1	197.4
	Total (NPV)	350	106.0	–80.6

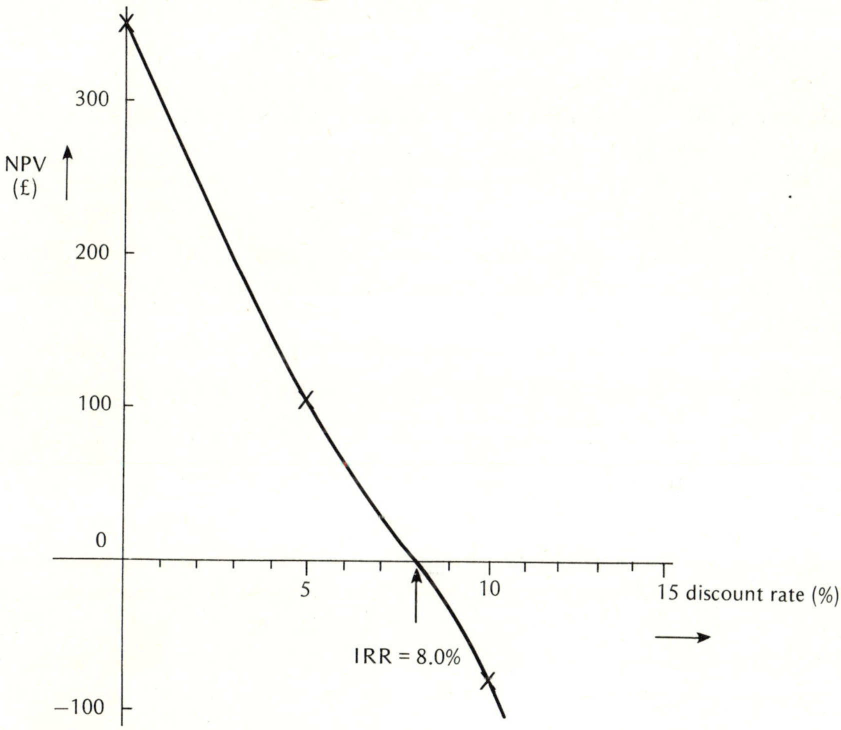

Fig. 6.1 *Calculation of internal rate of return.*

greater than the IRR, the NPV will be negative (and hence the project should be rejected), while if the discount rate is less than the IRR, the NPV will be positive (and hence the project should be accepted). We can use this fact to establish a simple rule for accepting or rejecting projects: given a discount rate (which in this context could be called a 'desired rate of return'), the project should be accepted if its IRR is greater than the discount rate, and rejected if its IRR is less.

The above rule does not, of course, completely resolve the problem of choosing a discount rate (or desired rate of return), although it does somewhat lessen its importance. For example, if we think that the appropriate discount rate lies somewhere between 10 and 15 per cent, but are unable or unwilling to specify it precisely, we can still with confidence reject all those projects whose IRR is greater than 15 per cent.

Determining the Cut-off Level

A more general approach is illustrated in Fig. 6.2. Suppose a company has a number of possible investment projects, A, B, C, D . . ., and that these are listed in decreasing order of their IRR. The projects can then be represented as in Fig. 6.2(a) by a series of rectangles, where the height of each rectangle corresponds to the expected IRR, and the width of each rectangle corresponds to the amount of capital required for a particular investment. The area of the rectangle is, incidentally, a measure of the total value of the project. The rectangles are then arranged from left to right in decreasing order of height, as shown in Fig. 6.2(a). A smooth curve can be drawn to approximate the line formed by the tops of the rectangles. This curve (Fig. 6.2(b)) represents the diminishing marginal rate of return which the company can obtain on its capital investment.

A similar curve can be constructed to show the possibilities available to the company for raising capital for investments. Typically, the company may have a small amount of capital available in cash (with zero cost of capital). The next most expensive possibility might be to use capital currently in a bank deposit account; the cost of this capital is the interest lost when the money is withdrawn from the account. When this cash is exhausted, the company can seek an overdraft, with a rather higher cost of capital; and finally perhaps can attract 'risk capital' at a high rate of interest. At each stage, the cost of capital increases, and this marginal cost of raising capital can be drawn as an increasing curve in Fig. 6.2(c). (Note that, while we have said that the more capital needed the higher will be the marginal cost of additional capital, it remains true that large companies may borrow large amounts of capital at lower interest rates than those charged for smaller sums to smaller companies. The curve in Fig. 6.2(c) represents the increasing marginal cost of capital *for a particular company*.)

The next step is to draw the marginal rate of return curve (Fig. 6.2(b)) and the marginal cost of capital curve (Fig. 6.2(c)) on the same scale, as in Fig. 6.2(d). Since the first curve is always decreasing and the second always increasing, the curves must intersect at point X. The interest rate i at which this intersection occurs is the point at which the cost of borrowing one additional pound is precisely equal to the return obtained on investing one additional pound. Hence, this interest rate represents the minimum IRR which the company can accept as profitable, and all projects to the left of the intersection point should be accepted while all those to the right are rejected.

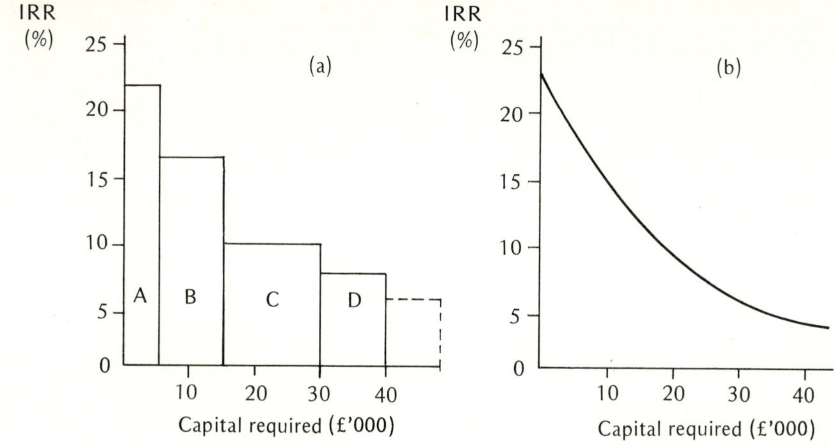

Project	Capital required (£)	IRR (%)
A	5 000	22
B	10 000	16
C	15 000	10
D	16 000	8
↓	↓	↓
↓	↓	↓
↓	↓	↓

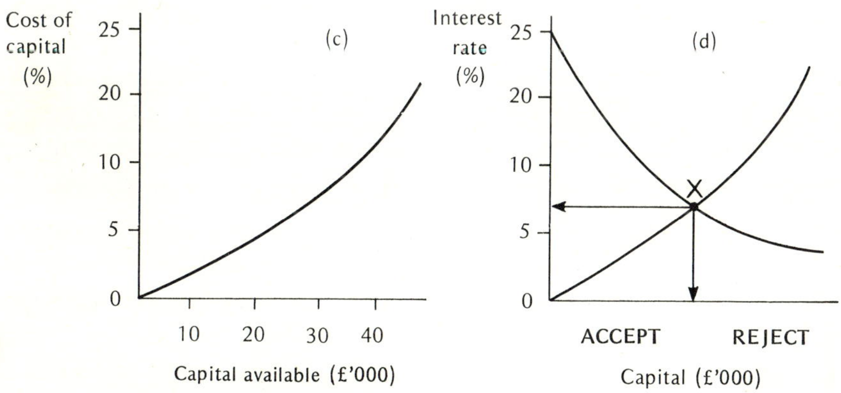

Fig. 6.2 *A general method for determining the IRR cut-off level.*

This procedure gives a rule for determining the cut-off level for IRR in deciding whether or not to accept or reject a given project. One special case is worth pointing out: if the company has only one cost of capital, and can raise as much money as it requires at the same cost, then the marginal cost of capital 'curve' becomes a horizontal straight line (see Fig. 6.3). In this case the rule is reduced to the obvious: accept those projects with a higher IRR than the cost of capital, and reject those with a lower IRR.

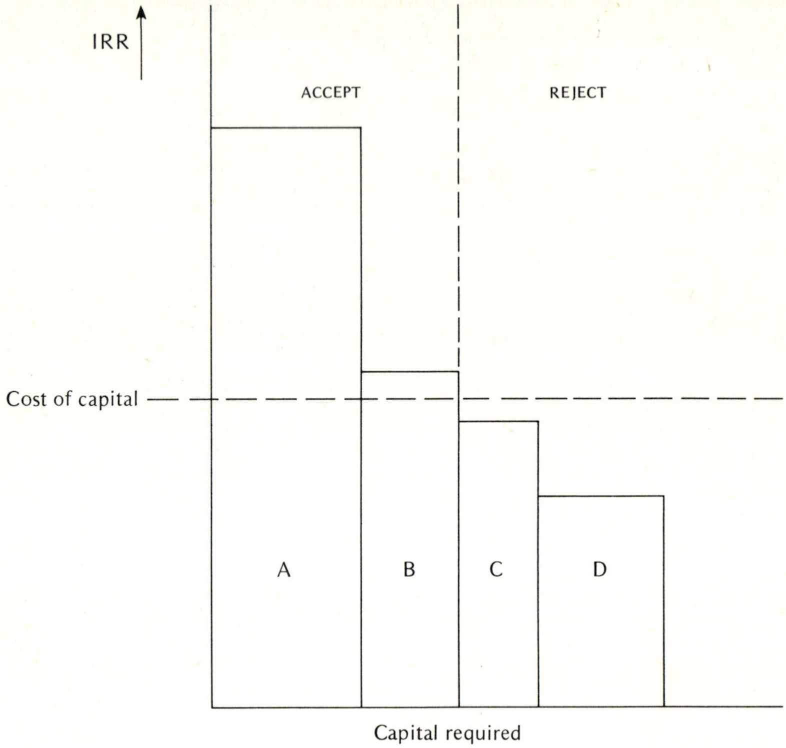

Fig. 6.3 *A special case: constant cost of capital.*

IRR EVALUATED

In chapter 4 we enumerated four tests which a technique for capital investment appraisal ideally should pass. To obtain a critical assessment of IRR as a means of capital investment appraisal, we shall see how it measures up to these four criteria.

- It should be unambiguous. While IRR is, as we shall see, in many respects the best single criterion for appraising capital investment, it does have one unfortunate disadvantage: it is not always uniquely defined. Consider the following simple example.

Year	Cash flow (£)
0	–160
1	+1000
2	–1000

IRR = 25% or 400%

A project has an initial capital expenditure of £160 in year 0, producing a positive cash flow of £1000 in year 1. Further investment is required in year 2, producing a negative cash flow of £1000. It is not difficult to show that this project has an IRR of 25 per cent. Unfortunately, it turns out that an IRR of 400 per cent is also an equally good solution of the equation:

$$-160 + \frac{1000}{1+i} - \frac{1000}{(1+i)^2} = 0.$$

In this particular case it may be argued that 25 per cent is the 'right' IRR and 400 per cent the 'wrong' one, on the grounds that 25 per cent seems plausible while 400 per cent does not. Recall that the underlying assumption of DCF is that all capital is borrowed at some fixed rate of interest, while all excess earnings are invested at the same rate. While 25 per cent might be considered a plausible rate either for cost of capital or for interest on other investments, 400 per cent would certainly not be. This can be extended to a more general rule: where more than one possible IRR exists, use the smallest (positive) IRR. However, the moral is clear: in certain cases multiple values of IRR may exist, and great care should be exercised in interpreting these results. This question is further complicated by the fact that there is no general rule to enable the user to know whether a given project will produce more than one IRR. All that can be said is that if the project cash flows change sign only once (i.e., if all the cash flows prior to some time t are positive, and all those after time t are negative, or vice versa), then the IRR is uniquely defined. However, if the cash flows change sign more than once, it does *not* necessarily imply that the IRR is not unique.

- It should be consistent with intuition. On this count IRR works extremely well; it takes account of all the cash flows associated with the project, and of the time value of money. Furthermore, the IRR corresponds to the intuitive idea of 'rate of return on investment' better than any other single measure. Only when the IRR is extremely large (say 40 per cent or more) or negative (less than 0 per cent) does it become difficult to reconcile with intuitive ideas. It is scarcely necessary to point out that a project with an IRR of greater than 40 per cent is unlikely to be rejected, while a project with an IRR of less than 0 per cent is unlikely to be accepted. Hence, this departure from intuition does not pose a real problem in the use of IRR as a criterion for acceptance/rejection of capital projects.

- It should be widely applicable. There may be cases where the IRR is not uniquely defined, and this limits the scope of application of the technique, but IRR can be used unambiguously for the majority of projects, including all those where only one sign change occurs in the cash flow. In practice, the only types of project which are likely to produce serious difficulties are those with two or more substantial capital expenditures (i.e., large negative cash flows) at substantially different points in time. An example might be the development of an open-cast mine, where the countryside has to be restored when the mine is no longer worked. Even for such relatively unusual projects there will usually be one 'plausible' IRR, which can be taken as the 'correct' IRR, while the others can be ignored.

• It should be easy to use. While it is true that the calculation involved in using IRR is more complex than calculations involved in any of the other appraisal techniques thus far discussed, it cannot be called a major disadvantage. Even if a computer program is not available for performing the calculations, all that is involved, using the interpolation method depicted in Fig. 6.1, is the calculation of the NPV of the cash flows at three or four different trial discount rates. Assuming that the calculator is provided with a set of discount tables, each NPV calculation requires one multiplication for each year of the project. Once the calculation is performed the IRR has the very great advantage, referred to above, that it has a readily interpretable intuitive meaning: in a very real sense a project with an IRR of 20 per cent uses its capital twice as profitably as a project with an IRR of 10 per cent.

IRR and Cost of Capital

In chapter 2 we defined three different sources of capital: internally generated capital, loans, and equity issues. The IRR technique described above provides a realistic method for determining cost of capital raised by loans or equity issues.

Consider all the cash flows associated with making a loan or with an equity issue: cash *in* to the company as loan or subscription for equity and cash *out* as interest, loan repayments and dividends. These cash flows could be considered as belonging to a capital investment project for the provider of the loan or purchaser of the new equity, and an associated internal rate of return can therefore be calculated. This IRR is the effective interest paid on the loan/equity issue, and hence is the appropriate discount rate to use in NPV calculations where the anticipated source of capital is from loans or an equity issue.

Unfortunately, no such conceptually sound technique exists for calculating the cost of internally generated capital. The best general rule that can be given is that the discount rate used should be the best interest rate obtainable on an alternative use of the same capital. For example, if the capital would otherwise lie in a bank account earning 5 per cent the 5 per cent is the appropriate cost of capital. If, alternatively, there exist many small projects which would bring in an average return of 15 per cent, then 15 per cent is the appropriate cost of capital.

In practice, it is often difficult to say precisely which part of the capital is used for which investment. One approach to this problem is to take a weighted average of the capital costs of the different components. For example, if a company has £5000 of internally generated capital available, at an estimated capital cost of 5 per cent, and proposes to borrow a further £3000 at 10 per cent, the appropriate discount rate would be the weighted cost of two capital components:

$$\frac{(3000 \times 10) + (5000 \times 5)}{8000} = \frac{55}{8} = 6.87\%.$$

Profitability Index

same NPV but different capital.

One of the disadvantages of NPV is that, used alone, it does not provide sufficient information to enable projects to be ranked in order of preference. For example, two projects each having a NPV of £1000 may require radically different amounts of capital: say £300 for one project, and £500 for the other. Since NPV is a measure of total value to the company of all the cash flows associated with the project, it is obviously preferable to select the first, which only requires £300 capital outlay to produce a net return of £1000, rather than the second, which requires an outlay of £500.

What is required is some method of relating the NPV of the cash flows to the total capital required for the project. One way of achieving this is by using the IRR, as described on pp. 53–55. An alternative way is to use the co-called 'profitability index' (PI). This is defined simply as the ratio of the net present value of the project to the total capital expenditure. In the case where all the capital expenditure occurs in year 0 (i.e., total capital expenditure = C_0), the profitability index is therefore defined by:

$$\text{PI} = \frac{NPV}{C_0} = \frac{1}{C_0} \sum_r \frac{C_r}{(1+i)^r}.$$

For the more general case where capital expenditures may constitute parts of the cash flows in several years, suppose that E_r is the total capital expenditure in year r. The PI is then defined as the ratio of the NPV of *all* the cash flows to the NPV of the capital expenditures. In algebraic form:

$$\text{PI} = \frac{\sum_r \frac{C_r}{(1+i)^r}}{\sum_r \frac{E_r}{(1+i)^r}}.$$

The use of the profitability index very much simplifies the decision-making procedure: any project with a PI greater than 1 should be accepted, while any project with a PI of less than 1 should be rejected. If the choice is between two mutually exclusive projects, the project with the higher PI is considered preferable.

Thus, in the example above the first project would have a PI of 1000/300 = 3.3, while the second has a PI of 1000/500 = 2.0. PI is often used in conjunction with NPV to resolve this kind of choice.

NPV and IRR Using Two Discount Rates

In discussing the underlying principles of DCF (see p. 44), we mentioned the basic assumption of a perfect capital market, where any sum of money always can be invested or borrowed at the same interest rate. In practice, these two rates are always different, and for NPV calculations the problem is to decide the appropriate rate to select. One solution is to take the cost of capital or borrowing cost if the company is not acpital constrained, and the opportunity cost (i.e., rate of return available on alternative investments) in the case where the company is capital constrained.

A method which largely overcomes these problems, although at the cost of some complexity, has been developed by Teichroew Robichek and Montalbano (see Bibliography, 12). In view of the relative complexity of the technique we shall only discuss the general principles here.

The basic idea is to use two separate discount rates, one representing the cost of borrowing capital (borrowing rate), and the other the return available on investing capital (lending rate). If, at the end of a year, the NPV of the total cash flows to date is negative, the project is said to be in debt, and the cash flow for the next year is discounted at the borrowing rate. Conversely, if the NPV of the cash flows to date is positive, the project is said to be in credit and hence the next year's cash flow is discounted at the lending rate.

Formally, if C_r is the cash flow in year r, and i and j are the borrowing and lending rates respectively, $P(i,j)$ is the NPV using two discount rates. In order to calculate $P(i,j)$ we need to define an intermediate variable $P_r(i,j)$, which is the NPV using two discount rates of the first r years' cash flows. If the last year of the project is year n, we then have:

$$P_0(i,j) = C_0$$

and for $r = 1, 2, \ldots n$

$$D_0 = 1$$

$$D_r = \frac{D_r - 1}{1 + i} \text{ if } P_{r-1} < 0$$

$$D_r = \frac{D_{r-1}}{1-j} \text{ if } P_{r-1} > 0$$

$$P_r = P_{r-1} + C_r D_r$$

and finally

$$P(i,j) = P_n.$$

(D_r is the (mixed) discount factor used to discount the cash flow in year r back to year 0.)

If the function $P(i,j)$ is regarded as a generalization of the NPV, similar generalizations can be obtained for the IRR. If we fix either i or j, the equation $P(i,j) = 0$ can be solved for the other discount rate. This gives two generalizations of the IRR, called in the article just mentioned the 'project financing rate' and the 'project investment rate'. It may be shown that the use of these generalizations can eliminate problems of uniqueness and ambiguity; furthermore, it is possible to develop a set of consistent rules for applying these techniques to any project.

WHICH METHOD SHOULD BE USED?

In this chapter and in chapters 4 and 5, we have reviewed each of the major methods for appraising capital investment projects: payback, rate of return, NPV, IRR, PI and extensions thereof. If the reader thinks he has detected in the analyses a bias against non-DCF methods he is perfectly correct. It is the author's view that any technique for capital investment appraisal which is not based on the principles of discounted cash flow is unsatisfactory. The advantages of DCF methods and the shortcomings of non-DCF methods are so clear as to render further consideration of non-DCF methods a waste of time.

There remains the problem of which of the several DCF-based techniques we have discussed is preferable. The generalizations using two discount rates, despite their theoretical attractions, are probably too complex for regular use. We are left therefore with three possible techniques: NPV, IRR, and PI. Weston and Brigham (see Bibliography, 7) list six situations under which the use of NPV, IRR, and PI may produce different project rankings, and hence different decisions:

1. the cash flow of one project increases, while that of the other decreases;
2. the projects have significantly different lives;
3. the cost of one project is substantially larger than that of the other;

4. investment opportunities in the future are expected to be substantially different from the present, and the direction of change (better or worse) is known;
5. the firm is making investments at such a high rate that the marginal cost of capital curve (see Fig. 6.2(c)) is rising rapidly;
6. the firm is significantly capital constrained.

Provided that none of these conditions exists, the three methods will produce the same result; consequently it is of no importance which is used. If one or more of the conditions do hold, then problems may arise; and unfortunately there are no universal rules for what to do.

For the simplified approach in this book we offer the following general advice:

(a) Calculate the values of all three criteria for every project. If they all lead to the same decision there is no problem.
(b) If they do not lead to the same decision, NPV and/or PI is generally more reliable if the company is not capital constrained; IRR is generally more reliable if the company is capital constrained.
(c) If you must use one criterion only, use IRR.

For a more extensive analysis of the relative advantages and disadvantages of the different methods, the reader is advised to turn to the book by Weston and Brigham.

Checklist

1. Can you give examples of projects which are (a) probably suitable, and (b) probably unsuitable for appraisal with IRR?
2. What are the main advantages and disadvantages of IRR, PI, and NPV with two discount rates? Which would you consider the most appropriate:
   (a) For government decisions?
   (b) For personal decisions?
   (c) For decisions in your company?

7
Risk and uncertainty

In chapter 4, we divided capital investment appraisal problems into four categories, depending on whether the cash flows were determined with certainty or not, and whether the projects were mutually independent or interdependent. In chapters 5 and 6 the discussion was restricted to the simplest case: the project cash flows were known with certainty, and the projects were independent. Here we consider the case where projects remain independent, but where the cash flows cannot be forecast with certainty. The general characteristics of the problem are discussed and several techniques described which, with varying degrees of success, have been developed to deal with this problem.

WHAT ARE RISK AND UNCERTAINTY?

It is customary, in the literature on financial decision-making, to differentiate between 'risk' and 'uncertainty'. Uncertainty is said to exist whenever the cash flows associated with a project cannot be predicted exactly, while risk is said to exist when the uncertainty is sufficient that it might lead to a decision being made which, in the light of subsequent events, turns out to have been incorrect.

Consider, for example, two projects A and B; the IRR of project A may be anywhere between 20 per cent and 40 per cent, while that of project B may be anywhere in the range 5 to 25 per cent, depending in each case on the various uncertainties inherent in the project. Suppose also that the company is capital constrained and estimates its average return available on alternative projects to be 15 per cent. In both projects there is obviously considerable uncertainty—a possible range of 20 per cent for the IRR for each project. There is, however, an important distinction between the two cases: in project A, even the 'worst' possible case—an IRR of 20 per cent—is significantly better than the opportunity cost of 15 per cent, while project B could turn out to have an IRR of less than 15 per cent (and thus should have been rejected). So, according to our definitions, project B involves risk as well as uncertainty, while project A involves uncertainty alone.

When discussing one project in isolation, our distinction between risk and uncertainty seems clear enough. In practice, however, a project can never be isolated completely from other factors. Implicit in the decision to accept project A, for example, may be the assumption that the profits are to be used for future investment in project B. Provisional decisions for project B may depend on whether project A produces 20 per cent or 40 per cent. Thus, the element of risk is never entirely absent from questions involving uncertainty. For this reason it seems somewhat arbitrary to distinguish between them, and henceforth the two words will be used interchangeably.

WHEN IS UNCERTAINTY A PROBLEM?

It is very rare for any future event in the business world to be known with certainty. We may know, thanks to philosophical theories of inductive reasoning, that the sun will rise tomorrow, but when man becomes involved such confidence in our predictions diminishes rapidly. Uncertainties in the forecasting of wages, retail and wholesale prices, consumer demand, strikes, and all the other ingredients which may go into the calculation of forecast cash flows for a capital investment project, make it virtually impossible ever to predict such cash flows exactly. Should one conclude, then, that the use of the techniques described in chapters 5 and 6 is pointless? Or alternatively that, since no one can predict the future, any kind of detailed analysis is useless? . . . Obviously not. First, the uncertainties may be sufficiently small as to be unlikely to affect the rectitude of the decision taken and, secondly, the future is never entirely unpredictable. At the very worst we know that whatever the income and expenditure of a given project, the profit is always equal to the difference between them—about this there is no uncertainty.

The problem, then, is to answer two questions:

(a) Is the uncertainty inherent in the forecast cash flows of a given project, or group of projects, such that it could lead to the 'wrong' decision being taken? Alternatively, is the uncertainty such that planning of other projects is made difficult because of interactions with the project(s) under consideration?

(b) If there is significant uncertainty, can we identify the principal sources of uncertainty, and minimize its effects on our decision-making?

Intuitive Methods

Probably the most widely used approach for dealing with problems of risk is to make a point forecast and then use intuitive judgement. The procedure is first to make a 'best estimate' forecast for each of the uncertain quantities (prices, wages, demand, etc.) and to use these forecasts as inputs for calculating the forecast cash flows; then, given the cast flows, the NPV and IRR of the project are calculated. These values are known as 'point forecasts' or 'best estimate' forecasts, and are of course the forecasts which would be produced by an analyst ignoring (or ignorant of) all uncertainties in his forecasting methods.

When the projects come up for decision, some intuitive ranking of the inherent risk involved is made. Thus, a project for cost reduction in the manufacturing process will normally be considered less risky than a project to launch a new product, while a project to increase production capacity will be considered less risky than an R & D project to develop a new process. Management intuitively weighs expected profit against risk and decides accordingly. For example, of two projects competing for the same amount of capital, a safe project with NPV of £5000 may be preferred to a more risky project with NPV of £6000. The actual decision will of course depend on such factors as the long-term policy of the company, its current and projected future earnings, and the relative numbers of safe and risky projects available.

A slightly more formal procedure is to use a 'risk-adjusted' discount rate. Under this procedure different discount rates are used for safe projects and for risky projects; cost reduction projects may use a discount rate of 10 per cent, while new product launches are discounted at 15 per cent, and R & D projects at 20 per cent. The NPVs of the different projects are then compared on an equal footing—obviously a project whose cash flows have been discounted at 20 per cent will have to produce substantially better incomes than a project whose cash flows have been discounted at 10 per cent, in order to produce a greater NPV.

The disadvantages of this type of analysis are evident: no account is taken of any detailed knowledge of the particular inaccuracies and uncertainties in each project. The decision to discount one project at 10 per cent and another at 15 per cent is arbitrary, as are the choices of the risk-adjusted discount rates. The best that can be said about this type of approach is that it does not ignore completely the problems of uncertainty.

Sensitivity Analysis

By far the most useful practical technique for dealing with problems of risk and uncertainty in capital investment appraisal (and in most other areas of decision-making) is the use of 'sensitivity analysis'. This is an approach, rather than a precisely defined technique, and as such is best explained by a few general comments and some illustrative examples.

The idea is very simple: for each major variable associated with a project, not merely the most likely value of the variable is specified, but also its upper and lower limits. Thus, a forecast of sales of 10 000 units for a new product in the first year of its launch might be supplemented by the additional information that sales will certainly not lie below 7500 units or above 12 500 units.

The cash flows which would result if these lower and upper limits were actually encountered are then calculated, so that we now have three sets of forecast cash flows for the project: one corresponding to our 'best estimate' point forecast (10 000 units), and one corresponding to each of the lower and upper limit forecasts (7500 units and 12 500 units respectively). We next calculate the values of the NPV (or IRR, etc. as appropriate) for each of these three sets of values. This gives a possible range of values for the NPV as a function of one variable.

Similar analyses may be performed with respect to other variables which cannot be forecast accurately (labour costs, raw material costs, etc.). Ideally, the NPV would be calculated for every possible combination of values of the different variables. Unfortunately, the number of cases to be considered rises rapidly with the number of variables (5 variables, with 3 possible values each, already gives a total of $3^5 = 243$ possible combinations, each requiring one possible case to be evaluated); thus it is often necessary (and sometimes sufficient) in practice to change only one variable at a time. This enables the most critical variables to be identified—those to which the NPV is most sensitive.

By this kind of analysis, the manager is enabled to study the results of accepting a project under different possible assumptions about future events. He can then decide whether the possible range of values of NPV is too great, or whether the possible lower values of NPV represent an acceptable risk for the company. Identification of critical variables enables further research to be concentrated on improving the accuracy of forecasts of those variables and, of course, on examining the possibility of reducing the sensitivity of the project NPV to those variables. These concepts are illustrated in the following example.

The STU company, which manufactures paper products for the domestic market, is considering whether to launch nationally a new improved paper tissue product. Because of the nature of the market it is difficult, even with the use of test market data, to forecast the total sales with any degree of accuracy. Estimates of the potential market share for the new product range from 5 per cent to 15 per cent with a most likely estimate of 10 per cent. A second source of uncertainty is the level of labour costs: management estimates that wage rates may increase as much as 25 per cent over the next two years, although it is possible that some of this could be saved through higher productivity. Labour costs could therefore be anywhere between the present forecasts and 20 per cent higher.

The first stage is to calculate the NPV associated with the project using each of the six predictions of the uncertain variables: three possible sales levels and two possible labour cost levels. This produces the following table.

Forecast NPV of project (£'000)

		Sales level		
		low (5%)	medium (10%)	high (15%)
Labour costs	present	160	250	350
	increased by 20%	150	235	330

From this information we can immediately draw two conclusions:

(a) NPV is not very sensitive to labour costs—it is unlikely that an error in forecasting labour costs would lead to the 'wrong' decision being made (i.e., a decision which would have been different, had the true cost of labour been known in advance). Thus, the inaccuracies in forecasts of labour costs are not likely to be a source of error and can probably be ignored.

(b) NPV is highly sensitive to market share—a 5 per cent market share or a 15 per cent market share produce respectively 36 per cent below and 40 per cent above the NPV of a 10 per cent share. This may indicate that further research (i.e., more extensive test marketing or market research), which would help to improve the accuracy of the market share estimate, would be justified.

ALTERNATIVE STRATEGIES AND REGRET MATRICES

A development of the present type of analysis involves the concept of 'regret matrices', which can be illustrated by an extension of the above example. Suppose that on the basis of the above analysis the following decisions are made:

(a) The possibility of radical increases in labour costs is highly unlikely to affect this decision, and will therefore not be considered further in this context.

(b) In view of the paramount importance of forecasting market share accurately, and the difficulty of achieving this, it may be of interest to look at strategies other than the one originally considered.

The first question to ask is: If the company knew that the market share would be 5 per cent, how much money could be saved by modifying the project strategy? Such modification might involve purchasing less capital equipment, and so on. Suppose that £30 000 could be added to the NPV of the project by this 'low' strategy, raising it to £190 000. A similar investigation yields a 'high' strategy, corresponding to certain knowledge of a 15 per cent market share, with a NPV of £390 000. In tabular form we can represent this information as follows.

		Sales level (*£'000s*)		
		low (5%)	medium (10%)	high (15%)
Strategy	low	190		
	medium (original project)	160	250	350
	high			390

The next question is self-evident: what would happen if we followed the 'low' strategy (or the 'high' strategy) and were wrong about the market share forecast? In other words, what are the missing entries in the table? Presumably, in the event of choosing the low strategy and achieving 10 per cent or even 15 per cent market share, the remaining market requirements would have to be manufactured elsewhere. This would be more expensive than for the medium or high strategies—since, by definition, these were assumed to be the best strategies for a 10 per cent and 15 per cent market share respectively. Similarly, we can calculate the effects of choosing the high strategy and being wrong. These calculations enable us to produce the completed table; such a table is also known as a 'pay-off matrix'.

		Sales level (*£'000s*)		
		low	medium	high
Strategy	low	190	235	290
	medium	160	250	350
	high	140	220	390

We now have all the information necessary to construct the 'regret' matrix. This matrix shows, for each combination of possible strategy and possible outcome, the greatest possible 'loss' to be incurred by selecting that strategy. Thus, if the low strategy were selected and the high sales level achieved, the resulting NPV would be £290 000; if the 'correct' decision (the high strategy) had been made, the NPV would have been £390 000. Therefore, £100 000 has been 'lost'. Similar calculations produce the following table of 'regret'.

		Sales level (*£'000s*)		
		low	medium	high
Strategy	low	0	15	100
	medium	30	0	40
	high	50	30	0

The three numbers in each row of the table show the 'regret' associated with picking the strategy corresponding to that row. 'Regret' is defined as the difference in pay-off (NPV in this case) between the result of the strategy chosen and the result of the best possible strategy for that outcome. Thus, if the low strategy is chosen and the high sales level results, the pay-off is only £290 000, whereas if the best strategy (high) had been chosen the pay-off would have been £390 000; the regret associated with the low strategy and the high sales level is therefore £390 000 – £290 000 = £100 000.

Given the two tables above, the decision-maker is provided with all the information necessary for evaluation of the alternative strategies and their associated risks. The analysis assumes that he has no quantitative information about the relative likelihoods of the different outcomes (the use of probability theory taking into account such information will be discussed in the final part of this chapter). He can weigh possible gains and possible losses against each other and decide on the appropriate amount of risk the company should take.

This procedure—the development of pay-off and regret matrices—is very little more than a formalization of the usual informal procedures by which managers make (or should make) decisions. This should be regarded as a strength of the present procedure rather than a weakness; the usefulness of this approach lies precisely in that it forces the decision-maker to complete the pay-off matrix by examining the consequence of being wrong as carefully as the consequences of being right.

It is worth mentioning briefly two of the more interesting of the many formal decision criteria proposed for making decisions of the type described above. While these criteria may be considered too simple for most real-life decisions, they are certainly useful concepts.

Maximin consists of selecting that strategy which *guarantees* the best possible lower limit for the NPV. In the example above the low strategy guarantees a pay-off of at least £190 000, while the medium and high strategies guarantee pay-offs of at least £160 000 and £140 000 respectively. Under this criterion, then, the low strategy would be chosen. This is obviously the most conservative choice.

Minimax regret consists of selecting that strategy which *guarantees* the smallest upper limit for the 'regret'. Thus, in the example, the regret associated with the low strategy will be no worse than £100 000, while the maximum regrets for the medium and high strategies would be £40 000 and £50 000 respectively. The decision-maker would, therefore, choose the medium strategy. This procedure has considerable intuitive appeal—since it picks that strategy which tries to minimize the amount of error.

PROBABILITY AND DECISION THEORY

The remainder of this chapter assumes an understanding of the elementary concepts of probability theory. The reader who is unfamiliar with these concepts should omit these pages, which are not necessary for an understanding of chapter 8.

We have so far avoided any mention of the concept of 'probability'. It has seemed logical initially to discuss techniques which do not use probability theory (and are thus conceptually simpler); and, in any event, there is considerable scepticism about the value of probability theory in investment decision-making. Almost all applications of probability theory to real-life decision-making require the estimation of prior, or subjective, probabilities. Unfortunately, decision-makers (whether lay managers or professional operations researchers) are extremely bad at estimating probabilities—with a strong tendency to over-optimism! Because of this, the use of methods such as those described here and in the section on simulation should be undertaken only with the greatest of care, and when sensitivity analysis has already yielded all it can.

Having criticized the methods, it should now be pointed out that there is one type of problem where methods involving the concept of probability can be of considerable use: when a company is faced with a very large number of investment decisions—e.g., a pharmaceutical company considering hundreds of possible new products every year. Such cases have one important characteristic: there is enough data on successes and failures of previous projects to produce estimates of probability substantially less subjective than would be the case for, say, a small company considering ten new products a year of which two are actually commissioned.

To illustrate the application of the simplest type of 'probabilistic' method we return to the example discussed in the last section and suppose that the market researcher on whose estimates the 'low', 'medium', and 'high' sales forecasts are based is asked to estimate the probabilities of each of these outcomes. His estimated probabilities of the different outcomes are 0.3, 0.5, and 0.2 respectively. In other words, he thinks that there is a 30 per cent chance of the new product achieving a 5 per cent market share, a 50 per cent chance of a 10 per cent market share, and a 20 per cent chance of a 15 per cent market share.

We can now calculate the expected pay-off corresponding to each strategy. If we select the low strategy, we have a 30 per cent chance of a pay-off of £19 000, a 50 per cent chance of £235 000, and a 20 per cent chance of £290 000. The expected pay-off is therefore:

$$190\,000 \times 0.3 + 235\,000 \times 0.5 + 290\,000 \times 0.2 = £232\ 500$$

Similarly, the expected pay-off for the medium strategy is:

$$160\,000 \times 0.3 + 250\,000 \times 0.5 + 350\,000 \times 0.2 = £243\ 000$$

and for the high strategy:

$$140\,000 \times 0.3 + 220\,000 \times 0.5 + 390\,000 \times 0.2 = £230\ 000.$$

Note that the *expected* pay-offs are in no case the same as the *most likely* pay-offs, which are respectively £235 000, £250 000 and £220 000. If expected pay-off is considered the best criterion to use for the decision, then clearly the medium strategy is significantly better than either of the others.

Unfortunately, the use of even this simple type of decision theory can raise more complex problems. If the project is a major one, expected pay-off may lead to unrealistic conclusions, as in the following example.

A company has to choose one of two projects, A and B; Project A guarantees (with 100 per cent probability) a NPV of £90 000, while project B has two possible outcomes—a 10 per cent probability of a NPV of £1 000 000, and a 90 per cent of a NPV of £0. The expected pay-offs are respectively £90 000 and £100 000, but most managers would prefer a certain £90 000 to a 10 per cent chance of £1 million. This kind of problem has led to much interesting research, beyond the scope of this book. This example does, however, serve to illustrate a type of problem which can arise from using probability and decision theory carelessly.

Simulation

In the example described in the preceding sections we assumed that there are only two factors which cannot be forecast accurately—labour costs and sales level. Of these one was subsequently ignored, because it turned out that the NPV was not very sensitive to uncertainty in that factor.

Unfortunately, many real-life projects have a number of components subject to considerable uncertainty, and the complexities of the different possible interactions between these components may be such that it is not possible to carry out the kind of sensitivity analysis described above. One approach, which has been used with some success, is the use of computer simulation or 'Monte Carlo' methods.

To illustrate the Monte Carlo technique, consider again the example of the previous section, in which a company is considering the launch of a new product. In addition to uncertainties in the forecasts of sales level and labour costs, suppose that substantial uncertainties exist in the forecasts of capital required and raw material costs. For each of these four variables a probability distribution can be constructed showing the relative likelihood of the different possible outcomes. These are shown in Fig. 7.1.

The simulation procedure (usually using a computer program) takes for each of the uncertain variables one value, selected according to the given probability distribution for each variable, and then uses those values to calculate a corresponding value for the IRR, NPV, or whatever criterion the decision-maker wishes to use. This procedure is repeated many times, and the different values obtained are used to construct a probability distribution for the IRR (see Fig. 7.1(e)). For example, it is clear above that the IRR will be somewhere between 2 per cent and 19 per cent with an expected value (mean) of 11 per cent. There is a 25 per cent chance of an IRR of less than 5 per cent, and a 25 per cent chance of an IRR greater than 15 per cent. This distribution (see project A, Fig. 7.2) may be compared with the distributions for other projects and the decision to accept or reject the project based on their distributions. For example, either project B or project C would clearly be preferred to project A, while the choice between B and C depends on the decision-maker's attitude to risk.

While simulation has the advantage of taking account of all the uncertainties inherent in a project, it has two serious drawbacks. First, as with any other method of decision theory, it is necessary to provide as input data probability distributions for all uncertain

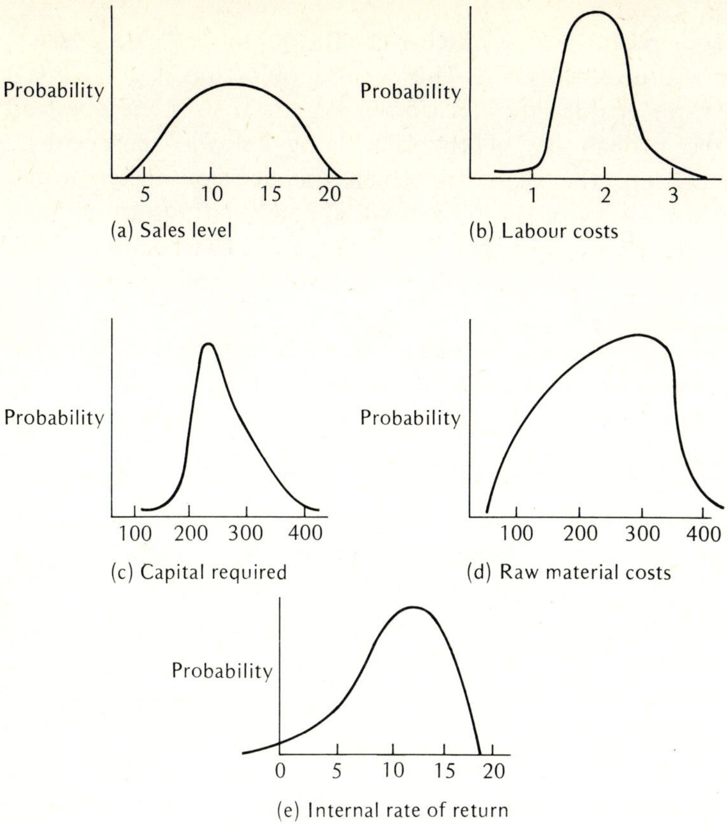

Fig. 7.1 *Examples of use of simulation.*

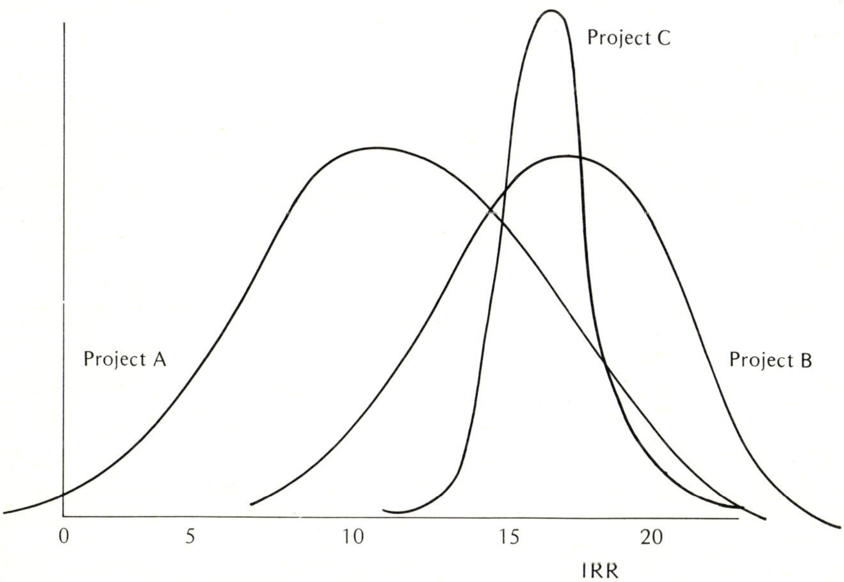

Fig. 7.2 *Probability distributions for different projects.*

variables, and except where extensive data on similar past projects are available this is difficult. The second objection is a technical one: simulation enables the decision-maker to answer the question 'What is the probability of the IRR lying below 7 per cent?', but unfortunately the question which the decision-maker would usually prefer answered is 'Under what combinations of circumstances will the IRR be less than 7 per cent, and can I do anything to avoid those cases?'—a question which simulation cannot answer.

Checklist

1. Construct an example of a 'risky' capital project, and identify the parameters to which the NPV is most sensitive.
2. Explain the basic principles of sensitivity analysis, and analyse its advantages and disadvantages.
3. What sort of projects would be particularly appropriate for using (i) 'maximum' and (ii) 'minimax regret' decision rules?
4. Why can the use of probabilities be misleading?

8
Company models

In the preceding chapters we have discussed ways of dealing with the case of independent projects, both under certainty and under uncertainty. Here we look at the case where the projects are not independent, and examine the use of company models—both specific and general—to analyse the problem.

INTERDEPENDENT PROJECTS

In classifying investment problems into four categories, we posed the question: Can the decision to accept or reject a particular project be made independently of the decision to accept or reject any other project? If the answer to this question is 'No', then the projects are said to be 'interdependent'.

In order to discuss the various techniques which can help to resolve problems involving interdependent projects, it is useful to distinguish between two types of interdependency: internal, and external. Two projects are said to be *internally* interdependent if the decision to accept or reject one of the projects actually affects the cash flows of the other. For example, suppose a company is considering installing a new production line in each of two neighbouring plants. An additional generator has to be provided if either of the production lines is installed, but the same generator will suffice for both. Obviously, if either one of the projects is accepted without the other, the cash flows for that project must include the capital and operating costs of the generator. If both projects are accepted, the costs associated with the generator could either be assigned to one of the projects, or divided between them. In either case, the cash flows associated with one of the projects will be affected by the acceptance or rejection of the other—the two projects are therefore internally interdependent.

Interdependence of this type exists to some degree in most projects. There are almost always some economies of scale to be realized in accepting more than one project, and there will therefore be some degree of interdependence in the project cash flows. However, where the interdependence is small, it can frequently be (and almost invariably is) ignored without serious consequence. Where the interdependence is substantial, as in the example described above, this approach will not suffice and more sophistication is required. The most effective way to solve the problem is to calculate three separate sets of cash flows, corresponding to the three acceptance possibilities: accept the first project and reject the second (A), accept the second project and reject the first (B), and accept both projects (C). (The fourth alternative, reject both projects, will of course have zero cash flows in all years.) These three cash flows can now be regarded as defining three new mutually independent projects A, B, and C, corresponding to the three alternative acceptance decisions. The problem has now been reduced to the following: select either one or none of the *three* alternative projects A, B, and C. This is a problem which can be solved by using the standard DCF technique for independent projects (since our definitions imply that A, B, and C are at least internally independent).

The above approach works well for two or three interdependent projects, but where the number of projects becomes large, the number of possible combinations becomes very large; 10 interdependent projects would generate 1023 new mutually exclusive projects—a lot of calculation. For such situations, the only satisfactory method of solution is to construct special computer models of the company. This technique will be discussed below.

The second type of interdependence is called 'external'. Two projects are defined as *externally* interdependent where financial (or operating) constraints external to the projects cause the decision to accept one project to preclude acceptance of the other. For example, where only enough production capacity is available for one of two new products to be launched, then the projects are externally interdependent. Alternatively, where a particular project requires a large amount of operating expenditure in year 2, which makes it impossible to start a second project in that year, the projects are again externally interdependent. It should be noted that projects may, of course, be both externally and internally interdependent.

Probably the most common example of externally interdependent projects arises from the situation known as 'capital rationing'. This occurs when a company has only a limited amount of capital available (or obtainable) and has to decide to which projects the capital should be allocated. In this situation the acceptance of any one project will use up some of the available capital and may therefore prevent the acceptance of some other project; all the projects, then, are externally interdependent. We now discuss some general techniques for dealing with this type of problem.

One of the most powerful techniques for assisting decision-makers faced with complex strategic problems in general, and complex capital investment appraisal problems in particular, is the use of a computerized financial model of the company. A model, reduced to barest essentials, is a set of logical statements which together constitute a complete financial description of those portions of the company's operations in which the decision-maker is interested. This set of statements, arranged as a computer program, enables the computer to calculate extremely rapidly what will happen to the company under any given set of circumstances, assuming, of course, that the financial description of the company inherent in the model is accurate.

It is important to realize that no magical ingredient is added to the model by transferring it to a computer. All the computer does is to perform calculations that could equally well have been carried out by a team of accounts clerks armed with desk calculators—the output of the computerized model is just as dependent on the input (forecasts of costs, revenue, etc.), and on the accuracy of the logical description of the company, as much as the team of clerks (actually more so, since a clerk will probably have the intelligence to recognize any inconsistencies or illogical assumptions inherent in the calculations). What the computer can do is to carry out the calculations much more rapidly and accurately than a team of clerks. If the managing director asks the question 'What will our earnings look like over the next five years if sales increase at 10 per cent per year and the price of raw material remains steady?', the team of clerks would require a few hours to produce the answers, while the computer takes a few seconds. If now the supplementary questions are asked 'What if the sales increase at 8 per cent or 12 per cent, and the raw material costs go up by 5 per cent next year and by a further 7 per cent two years later?', the computer model can produce the answers again in seconds, while posing the same questions to the team of clerks may immobilize the entire accounts department for days.

The speed with which the decision-maker can obtain the forecast results of a particular strategy or set of circumstances is not only useful in itself, but has an extremely important consequence: decision-makers are encouraged to ask questions, such as those above, thereby minimizing the danger of not having foreseen and prepared for a particular set of circumstances. In other words, the saving in time makes possible a full and complete sensitivity analysis of the kind described in chapter 7.

Some models can be constructed so that they not only determine the consequences of a given course of action, but also select whichever course of action is 'best' according to specified criteria—

e.g., a model might select that set of feasible investment projects with the greatest total NPV. Models that carry out this additional process are called 'optimization' models, while those which only answer questions of the 'What would happen if . . .?' variety are known as 'simulation' models. It should be pointed out, however, that this distinction is not absolute: 'simulation' models usually embody a limited amount of optimization, while the use of 'optimization' models still requires sensitivity analysis; the only real difference is that the question posed to an optimization model will be ofthe form 'What would be the best strategy to adopt if . . .?'.

The logical statements which constitute the financial description of the company at the heart of the model will, of course, vary between companies. No two companies, or even two divisions of the same company, can be described in quite the same way, since every organization has unique characteristics. This means, at least in principle, that every decision-making unit (company, division, etc.) requires its own specially constructed model. Since the writing and implementation of computerized company models is an expensive procedure, the use of a separate specialized model for every set of decisions is usually uneconomic. A considerable amount of research has therefore been devoted to the development of general company models which, while not necessarily capable of representing every detail, can nevertheless be made to behave sufficiently closely to the behaviour of any particular company to be of very substantial value in decision-making. To illustrate the use of such a model, we now describe in some detail the model called 'CAPRI', which has been used by a number of companies in Europe and North America for capital investment appraisal.

Capri

CAPRI—an acronym for 'computerized analysis for programming investment'—is a general computer program for appraisal problems where substantial external interdependencies exist between the different projects. It is described here not as a complete solution to the problem, but as an illustration of the power of the general technique of computerized financial models.

The basic problem which CAPRI is designed to solve is the following: select the optimal sub-set of projects from a given list of possible projects, taking into account the amount of capital available from different sources at different times, and any other relevant (external) financial constraints. At the same time the program decides which of the available sources of capital should be used. This operation, together with a particular method of raising the capital, is (in the context of this model) called the 'selection of an investment plan'.

Some of the investment possibilities in a list of projects will provide alternative ways of achieving the same objective, and may thus constitute a set of alternatives from which to choose no more than one. For example, a company might wish to double the capacity of a given production line, and it could achieve this objective in several alternative ways:

(a) Introduce double-shift working.
(b) Build a second production line identical to the first.
(c) Scrap the existing line and construct a new line with double the capacity.

The company requires to select only one of these alternatives. In this section we shall restrict the word 'project' to mean the achievement of a given objective, such as doubling the capacity of a production line, and the word 'alternative' to any one of the (in general) several ways of achieving this objective.

When using CAPRI, a given investment alternative must always be completely accepted or completely rejected; if a half-way stage is in practice possible, this must be included separately in the list of alternatives for that particular project. In addition, unless the company has already decided that it will accept the project in any case, and has only included the project in the model because of its effect on possible ways of financing, a do-nothing alternative must be included for that project. Given these two conditions (which imply that the given alternatives for any one project are both exclusive and exhaustive), the selection of an investment plan is reduced to the choice of exactly one alternative for each project.

Table 8.1 contains a hypothetical example of a list of projects and their alternatives from which a company wishes to select an investment plan. Future costs and revenues are associated with each investment alternative, for example:

(a) Capital costs.
(b) Operating costs.
(c) Revenue.
(d) Depreciation.
(e) Residual value at the end of useful life.

The company must define such future costs and revenues either for every year in the useful life of the investment, or precisely for the first few years, and then give a general rule (constant, linear, or exponential) for subsequent years. In this latter case the program will automatically calculate the values for the remainder of the useful life of the investment. It should be noted, that, since we are now considering interactions between projects, it is no longer sufficient to talk about the marginal cash flows associated with each project. We have to specify all the actual costs and revenues, and leave it to the model to calculate the cash flows corresponding to a given investment plan.

Table 8.1 *Investment projects and their alternatives*

Project		Alternatives
Double production capacity of a given product	(a)	Introduce double-shift working
	(b)	Install new production line
	(c)	Scrap existing production line and build a new line with double capacity
Reduce stocks held	(a)	Install computerized stock control system
Reduce distribution costs	(a)	Replace part of lorry fleet
	(b)	Install computerized lorry scheduling system
	(c)	Both (a) and (b)
	(d)	Build rail siding and transfer goods to rail
Diversify into new product field	(a)	Manufacture product under licence
	(b)	Research project to develop competitive product
	(c)	Take over existing company

In drawing up a list of investment possibilities, it is obviously not sufficient for a company to consider merely those projects which would commence in year 1 of the period under consideration, since the necessity to make a given investment in subsequent years may preclude making certain investments in year 1. Thus, in theory at least, the list must include all possible investment projects over a future period of time sufficient that investments subsequent to that period will have no influence on investment decisions the company makes in year 1.

Normally a company cannot specify all its possible future investments, even over a relatively short period such as five years. To overcome this difficulty, the model has the facility to take into account for each year a certain total of possible residual investments which will bring in a specified rate of interest. This interest rate (which corresponds formally to the discount rate used in present value calculations) would usually be determined in practice by taking the average IRR obtained by the company on all the projects it accepts.

In chapter 2 we discussed the different possible sources of capital available to a company: internally generated capital, borrowings, and new equity issues. When using CAPRI, the decision-maker specifies in general terms what options are open to the company with respect to raising capital from each source; the program calculates the amount of capital available from each of these sources in each year of the period considered, and then determines how much the company should take from each. It carries out this calculation for each year successively, since the amount of investment capital raised by the company from each source in any one year depends on the state of the company in that year, and hence on the investment decisions that the company has taken during the preceding years.

The internally generated capital available each year for capital investment comprises after-tax profits, less dividends paid to shareholders, with depreciation added back. The model allows the dividends either to be considered constant, or to increase linearly, subject to there being sufficient net profits available in each year to pay the dividend.

The amount of money a company can borrow in any one year normally depends on the net assets of the company. In the model, different types of loan possibilities can be specified, each being characterized by the maximum obtainable loan of that type, the rate of interest payable, and the schedule of repayments. In addition, the company can impose overall constraints relating total debts to net assets, and relate certain types of loan to certain investment projects or alternatives. This latter type of constraint is, in many cases, particularly important, since a higher interest rate may be associated with projects involving greater risk; also certain types of loan (e.g., government loans) may be restricted altogether to certain types of projects.

Companies cannot make new equity issues in an arbitrary fashion, since there are practical constraints on how often fresh share capital can be raised. Political considerations, based on the current economic situation, or on the state of the stock market, may also influence the decision. The model assumes that the amount of any new equity issue is specified, and also a maximum frequency of issue. The program then decides whether to make such an issue, and if so at what date.

Having specified the financial constraints (i.e., the external interdependencies of the projects), it remains to define what is meant by the 'optimal' investment plan. In chapters 4, 5, and 6 several different possible criteria were defined for evaluating individual capital projects. One of these, NPV at a given discount rate, can be used equally well to evaluate an investment plan. The NPV of an investment plan can be defined simply as the sum of NPVs of the project alternatives which comprise the plan. An alternative approach, based on the idea that companies are more interested in long-term growth than in profits, is to select that plan which will generate the most growth over some period (10 years, for example), where growth is defined as the increase in the net asset value of the company over that period. Either criterion can be used—in each case the program selects that investment plan which maximizes the given criterion, subject to the given financial constraints.

Figure 2.1 showed the main cash flows that take place within a company. Essentially, the model represents the relationships shown in this diagram as a set of equations whose variables represent the different quantities in different years of the period under consideration. Integer 'zero one' variables are used to represent the acceptance or rejection of a given alternative of a given project (and also the issue or non-issue of new equity capital). The selection of an optimal investment plan can then be reduced to solving a well-known type of mathematical problem—a mixed integer linear program—whose solution can be found by standard techniques.

In summary, the object of CAPRI is to select the overall investment plan for the whole period under consideration which is considered 'best' according to a certain criterion. Although this plan covers the whole period, obviously the company will implement immediately only those decisions affecting year 1, and will normally re-use the program at frequent intervals to update the later portions of the plan to take account of more accurate information about the development of the selected projects and the company's future investment possibilities.

INTERDEPENDENT PROJECTS UNDER UNCERTAINTY

So far in this chapter, we have implicitly discussed only those techniques which deal with interdependent projects under conditions where all the relevant cash flows associated with every potential project are known with certainty. Since, as pointed out in chapter 4, this assumption is never true in practice, what happens to our use of company models when we admit to uncertainty in our knowledge of some of our forecast, and hence by implication admit to the risk of making a 'wrong' decision?

In principle, all the techniques described in chapter 7 for dealing with uncertainty in independent projects can be extended to problems involving interdependent projects, although the increased complexity of the problem will obviously increase the amount of computation necessary. Sensitivity analysis, in the author's opinion, is once again by far the most useful general technique for dealing with uncertainties. The use of a general model such as CAPRI will enable the decision-maker to identify those projects for which the uncertainty is important and those for which it is not. Thus, if, when varying the uncertain parameters (which may refer not only to project cash flows but also to loan possibilities, interest rates, etc.), a particular project alternative is always contained in the optimal investment plan, it can be assumed that the decision to accept or reject that project alternative is relatively insensitive to the uncertainties. If, conversely, a particular project alternative moves in and out of the optimal investment plan as the parameters are varied, it indicates that the corresponding accept/reject decision is highly sensitive to the uncertainties, and that further research aimed at reducing these uncertainties should be carried out.

The alternative approach through simulation using random number techniques is also possible. This can be carried out by running the model many times for different randomly chosen values of the uncertain parameters, selected according to given probability distributions. Alternatively, in some cases, this may be done by building probability generation procedures into the model directly. In either case the amount of computation necessary, already quite large for a model of the complexity of CAPRI, will increase very substantially. Because of this and the previously mentioned problem of collection of data for 'objective' decisions under uncertainty, there is usually little to be gained from this approach until all other methods have been fully exploited. This is not to imply that simulation should be regarded as a last resort when all other methods have failed, but rather that only a user already fully experienced in other simpler techniques is likely to be able to benefit from use of the more complex techniques.

Checklist

1. What is the difference between *external* and *internal* interdependence of projects? Illustrate with examples.
2. What can the use of a company model add to simpler methods of decision-making? Are there any disadvantages in using company models?

Appendix: Present value of £1 receivable at the end of each period

	Percentage									
Year	1	2	3	4	5	6	7	8	9	10
1	0.990	0.980	0.971	0.962	0.952	0.943	0.935	0.926	0.917	0.909
2	0.980	0.961	0.943	0.925	0.907	0.890	0.873	0.857	0.842	0.826
3	0.971	0.942	0.915	0.889	0.864	0.840	0.816	0.794	0.772	0.751
4	0.961	0.924	0.888	0.855	0.823	0.792	0.763	0.735	0.708	0.683
5	0.951	0.906	0.863	0.822	0.784	0.747	0.713	0.681	0.650	0.621
6	0.942	0.888	0.837	0.790	0.746	0.705	0.666	0.630	0.596	0.564
7	0.933	0.871	0.813	0.760	0.711	0.665	0.623	0.583	0.547	0.513
8	0.923	0.853	0.789	0.731	0.677	0.627	0.582	0.540	0.502	0.467
9	0.914	0.837	0.766	0.703	0.645	0.592	0.544	0.500	0.460	0.424
10	0.905	0.820	0.744	0.676	0.614	0.558	0.508	0.463	0.422	0.386
11	0.896	0.804	0.722	0.650	0.585	0.527	0.475	0.429	0.388	0.350
12	0.887	0.788	0.701	0.625	0.557	0.497	0.444	0.397	0.356	0.319
13	0.879	0.773	0.681	0.601	0.530	0.469	0.415	0.368	0.326	0.290
14	0.870	0.758	0.661	0.577	0.505	0.442	0.388	0.340	0.299	0.263
15	0.861	0.743	0.642	0.555	0.481	0.417	0.362	0.315	0.275	0.239
16	0.853	0.728	0.623	0.534	0.458	0.394	0.339	0.292	0.252	0.218
17	0.844	0.714	0.605	0.513	0.436	0.371	0.317	0.270	0.231	0.198
18	0.836	0.700	0.587	0.494	0.416	0.350	0.296	0.250	0.212	0.180
19	0.828	0.686	0.570	0.475	0.396	0.331	0.277	0.232	0.194	0.164
20	0.820	0.673	0.554	0.456	0.377	0.312	0.258	0.215	0.178	0.149
21	0.811	0.660	0.538	0.439	0.359	0.294	0.242	0.199	0.164	0.135
22	0.803	0.647	0.522	0.422	0.342	0.278	0.226	0.184	0.150	0.123
23	0.795	0.634	0.507	0.406	0.326	0.262	0.211	0.170	0.138	0.112
24	0.788	0.622	0.492	0.390	0.310	0.247	0.197	0.158	0.126	0.102
25	0.780	0.610	0.478	0.375	0.295	0.233	0.184	0.146	0.116	0.092
30	0.742	0.552	0.412	0.308	0.231	0.174	0.131	0.099	0.075	0.057
35	0.706	0.500	0.355	0.253	0.181	0.130	0.094	0.068	0.049	0.036
40	0.672	0.453	0.307	0.208	0.142	0.097	0.067	0.046	0.032	0.022

Year	Percentage									
	11	12	13	14	15	16	17	18	19	20
1	0.901	0.893	0.885	0.877	0.870	0.862	0.855	0.847	0.840	0.833
2	0.812	0.797	0.783	0.769	0.756	0.743	0.731	0.718	0.706	0.694
3	0.731	0.712	0.693	0.675	0.658	0.641	0.624	0.609	0.593	0.579
4	0.659	0.636	0.613	0.592	0.572	0.552	0.534	0.516	0.499	0.482
5	0.593	0.567	0.543	0.519	0.497	0.476	0.456	0.437	0.419	0.402
6	0.535	0.507	0.480	0.456	0.432	0.410	0.390	0.370	0.352	0.335
7	0.482	0.452	0.425	0.400	0.376	0.354	0.333	0.314	0.296	0.279
8	0.434	0.404	0.376	0.351	0.327	0.305	0.285	0.266	0.249	0.233
9	0.391	0.361	0.333	0.308	0.284	0.263	0.243	0.225	0.209	0.194
10	0.352	0.322	0.295	0.270	0.247	0.227	0.208	0.191	0.176	0.162
11	0.317	0.287	0.261	0.237	0.215	0.195	0.178	0.162	0.148	0.135
12	0.286	0.257	0.231	0.208	0.187	0.168	0.152	0.137	0.124	0.112
13	0.258	0.229	0.204	0.182	0.163	0.145	0.130	0.116	0.104	0.093
14	0.232	0.205	0.181	0.160	0.141	0.125	0.111	0.099	0.088	0.078
15	0.209	0.183	0.160	0.140	0.123	0.108	0.095	0.084	0.074	0.065
16	0.188	0.163	0.141	0.123	0.107	0.093	0.081	0.071	0.062	0.054
17	0.170	0.146	0.125	0.108	0.093	0.080	0.069	0.060	0.052	–
18	0.153	0.130	0.111	0.095	0.081	0.069	0.059	0.051	–	–
19	0.138	0.116	0.098	0.083	0.070	0.060	0.051	–	–	–
20	0.124	0.104	0.087	0.073	0.061	0.051	–	–	–	–
21	0.112	0.093	0.077	0.064	0.053	–	–	–	–	–
22	0.101	0.083	0.068	0.056	–	–	–	–	–	–
23	0.091	0.074	0.060	–	–	–	–	–	–	–
24	0.082	0.066	0.053	–	–	–	–	–	–	–
25	0.074	0.059	–	–	–	–	–	–	–	–

Year	Percentage									
	21	22	23	24	25	26	27	28	29	30
1	0.826	0.820	0.813	0.806	0.800	0.794	0.787	0.781	0.775	0.769
2	0.683	0.672	0.661	0.650	0.640	0.630	0.620	0.610	0.601	0.592
3	0.564	0.551	0.537	0.524	0.512	0.500	0.488	0.477	0.466	0.455
4	0.467	0.451	0.437	0.423	0.410	0.397	0.384	0.373	0.361	0.350
5	0.386	0.370	0.355	0.341	0.328	0.315	0.303	0.291	0.280	0.269
6	0.319	0.303	0.289	0.275	0.262	0.250	0.238	0.227	0.217	0.207
7	0.263	0.249	0.235	0.222	0.210	0.198	0.188	0.178	0.168	0.159
8	0.218	0.204	0.191	0.179	0.168	0.157	0.148	0.139	0.130	0.123
9	0.180	0.167	0.155	0.144	0.134	0.125	0.116	0.108	0.101	0.094
10	0.149	0.137	0.126	0.116	0.107	0.099	0.092	0.085	0.078	0.073
11	0.123	0.112	0.103	0.094	0.086	0.079	0.072	0.066	0.061	0.056
12	0.102	0.092	0.083	0.076	0.069	0.062	0.057	0.052	–	–
13	0.084	0.075	0.068	0.061	0.055	–	–	–	–	–
14	0.069	0.062	0.055	–	–	–	–	–	–	–
15	0.057	0.051	–	–	–	–	–	–	–	–

(Taken from Wright, M. G., *Discounted Cash Flow*, McGraw-Hill, 1967.)

Bibliography

Capital investment appraisal is a subject which has over the last decade generated a great many books and articles. This list therefore does not attempt to be comprehensive, but provides the reader interested in pursuing this and related subjects with a few sources of further information.

Books

1. Alfred, A. J. and Evans, J. B., *Discounted Cash Flow,* Chapman and Hall, 1966. A practical handbook on DCF as practised at Courtaulds.
2. Baumol, W. J., *Economic Theory and Operations Analysis,* Prentice-Hall, 1965. Contains an excellent analysis of risk and uncertainty, and a good survey of capital budgeting techniques.
3. Clarkson, G. P. E., *Managerial Finance,* Penguin Books, 1968. This collection of articles includes several on capital investment appraisal.
4. Merrett, A. J. and Sykes, A., *Capital Budgeting and Company Finance,* Longmans, Green & Co, 1966. Excellent, if relatively technical, condensed and updated version of their standard work.
5. Merrett, A. J. and Sykes, A., *The Finance and Analysis of Capital Projects,* Longmans, Green & Co, 1963. The standard English text.
6. Quirin, G. D. *The Capital Expenditure Decision,* Irwin, 1966. Entertainingly written, but fairly technical.
7. Weston, J. F. and Brigham, E. F., *Managerial Finance,* Holt, Rinehart, and Winston, 1969. Standard text on finance for first year MBA students; outstanding breadth of subject matter and very lucidly written.
8. Wright, M. G., *Discounted Cash Flow,* McGraw-Hill, 1967. A sound introduction to the subject.

Articles

9. Harrison, I. W., CAPRI, *Management Decision,* Spring, 1969. A little more detail on the model described in chapter 8.

10. Hertz, D. B., Risk analysis in capital investment, *Harvard Business Review,* January–February, 1964. Monte Carlo methods for capital investment appraisal.
11. Markowitz, H., Portfolio selection, *Journal of Finance,* March, 1952. A classic article on risk analysis in portfolio selection.
12. Teichroew, D., Robichek, A. A. and Montalbano, M., An analysis of criteria for investment and financing decisions under certainty, *Management Science,* November, 1965, 151–79. (Reprinted in Clarkson (above).) Covers DCF with two discount rates in some detail.

Other publications

13. H. M. Customs, *Customs and Excise Notices on VAT,* H.M.S.O., 1972. A series of booklets explaining in simple non-legal terms the essentials of the VAT system.

Index

Printed by William Clowes & Sons Limited, London, Colchester and Beccles